Reaching for a Star

REACHING FOR A STAR

The Final Campaign for Alaska Statehood

By Gerald E. Bowkett

EPICENTER PRESS
Alaska Book Adventures™
www.EpicenterPress.com

Photos on cover: top—President Dwight D. Eisenhower displays new forty-nine-star flag after signing the Alaska statehood proclamation on January 3, 1959. (E.L. "Bob" Bartlett Collection, Alaska Archives, University of Alaska Fairbanks); bottom—William A. Egan, president of the Alaska Constitutional Convention, signs the constitution on February 5, 1956. (Ralph J. Rivers Collection, Alaska Archives, University of Alaska Fairbanks)

Epicenter Press is a regional press publishing nonfiction books about the arts, history, environment, and diverse cultures and lifestyles of Alaska and the Pacific Northwest. For more information, visit www.EpicenterPress.com.

Publisher: Kent Sturgis
Acquisitions editor: Lael Morgan
Production editor: Sheryn Hara, Book Publishers Network
Cover design: Marc Robertson/Laura Zugzda
Printer: Lightning Source

Copyright ©1989, 2009 by Gerald E. Bowkett. All rights reserved. No part of this publication may be reproduced, stored in a retrieval system, or transmitted in any form or by any means, electronic, mechanical, photocopying, recording, or otherwise, without the prior written permission of the publisher. Permission is given for brief excerpts to be published with book reviews in newspapers, magazines, newsletters, catalogs, and online publications.

Library of Congress Control Number: 2009924729
ISBN 978-0-9800825-5-5

Trade Paperback original edition published in 1989 by Epicenter Press
2nd Edition, first printing, April 2008
10 9 8 7 6 5 4 3 2 1

Printed in the United States of America

To order single copies of this edition of REACHING FOR A STAR, mail $14.95 plus $6 for shipping (WA residents add $1.90 state sales tax) to Epicenter Press, PO Box 82368, Kenmore, WA 98028. Orders also may be placed by phone to 800-950-6663 or by visiting our website, www.EpicenterPress.com. Contact info@EpicenterPress.com regarding volume discounts.

To Norma

I remember well the atmosphere of the convention, a feeling that we were working on something that would have an everlasting impact on the future of the then Territory of Alaska and the new state-to-be. There was a feeling of something historic, of something that just had to be accomplished in a given period of time.
—William A. Egan
University of Alaska, Fairbanks
December, 1972

Contents

Foreword ix
Preface xi
Introduction 1
1 Getting Under Way 5
2 Why Statehood? 9
3 The Fight for Statehood 14
4 Organizing the Convention 20
5 Open or Closed Committee Meetings? 25
6 A One- or Two-House Legislature? 29
7 A New Capital? 34
8 Appoint or Elect Judges? 38
9 Voting Qualifications 42
10 Home for Christmas 46
11 Power to the People 49
12 Fish and Game Management 52
13 Land to Natives? 57
14 Local Government 60
15 The Legislature 64
16 Legislative Apportionment 68
17 A Strong Executive 70
18 Moving against the Traps 74
19 Pushing for Statehood 78
20 A Little Militancy 82
21 The Final Days 85
22 A Constitution for Alaska 88
23 Winning the Fight 93
Epilogue 101
Appendix 1: The Delegates 105
Appendix 2: The Alaska Constitution 107
Appendix 3: Amendments 147
Notes 150
Suggested Reading 156
Index 158

Foreword

EVEN WITHOUT THE ASSURANCE OF STATEHOOD, the fifty-five men and women who gathered in Fairbanks ion November of 1955 to craft Alaska's constitution had a clear view of what democracy is all about.

They were successful beyond anyone's wildest dreams in measuring thesocial and political needs of the 200,000 Alaskans who lived in the then Territory, and who would soon live in the state. Their foresight produced a document that has continued to adapt to new and different challenges, as Alaska has grown and stretched and come of age.

Just seventy years before the constitutional convention, Alaska was "Seward's icebox" to most of the nation. In the mid-1950s it was still viewed by many in the "South 48" as a place so distant that few Americans in their right mind would really choose to live there. Alaskans were definitely a people apart—there was widespread suspicion that Alaskans were too far-removed, too brash, too different to be entrusted with statehood and its responsibilities.

Yet the Alaska constitution, created by this isolated band of dreamers, has been hailed as the model for all state constitutions. It is certainly the most significant reaffirmation of the principles of the U.S. Constitution in this century.

The people of Alaska proved, through the creation and adoption of their constitution, that our democracy was, and is, the most vibrant the world has ever known.

Those of us who were fortunate enough to know the fifty-five men and women who drafted Alaska's constitution, and who watched the whole story of statehood unfurl, continue to marvel at our good fortune to be Alaskans. We've had a privilege granted to few Americans.

TED STEVENS

Preface

MOST AMERICANS TODAY could hardly imagine living under a government they had not elected. And phrases such as "no taxation without representation" and "government by consent of the governed" would likely seem ancient and musty, something dimly remembered from the history classes of their youth.

Yet to Alaskans who fought for statehood in the 1940s and 1950s they were highly charged and meaningful phrases, for territorial residents at that late date were still denied the basic rights inherent in them.

The Alaska Constitutional Convention of the mid-1950s was conceived as a means of advancing the statehood cause, and there can be little doubt that it rekindled hopes and sparked the final drive for statehood.

The convention was a miniature Alaska of that time, its delegates embodying the hopes, concerns, frustrations and idealism of their fellow Alaskans.

The verbatim day-to-day record of the convention plenary sessions—those sessions in which the full body discussed, debated and took final action on committee and individual proposals—reveals the delegates as a determined, individualistic, straightforward lot with strong convictions and given to strong, often colorful expression. My account is heavily based on that record, which was produced from tapes and runs to nearly 4,000 pages. Unless otherwise noted, the quotations used are from that source.

It is fortunate the plenary sessions were taped. Without those tapes much less would be known of the convention. Some of the written records and reports, mainly having to do with the work of the committees, were deposited at the University of Alaska following the convention and soon lost. The decision to tape the proceedings was arrived at only after lengthy discussion by the delegates, a number of whom worried about the cost.

My objective in writing this book was to tell the human story of the convention—to show through re-creation of some of the principal debates, using the delegates' own words whenever feasible, what kind of people they were, how they dealt with issues that came before them, and what it was like to participate in the drafting of Alaska's constitution.

Press accounts, primarily those of the *Fairbanks Daily News-Miner*, were essential to this recounting of the convention story. The *News-Miner*, utilizing Associated Press wires, provided convention coverage daily for radio and television stations as well as other newspapers around the Territory.

Victor Fischer's *Alaska's Constitutional Convention*, the basic work on that singular event written from the unique perspective of a convention delegate, provided valuable insights.

No work such as this can be completed without the assistance of many people. It has been my good fortune to know a number of the convention delegates and several at my request have talked with me over the years and responded to my questions about the convention. The late Bill Egan, always a man of the present reluctant to be classified a figure of history, patiently reminisced about those Fairbanks days on several occasions. His wife Neva has graciously helped to clarify several matters. Burke Riley, Eldor Lee (in remembering Egan), Steve McCutcheon and Katie Hurley, chief clerk of the convention, have generously shared their recollections of the time.

My wife, Norma Swain Bowkett, long a teacher of English, went over the manuscript with her expert eye and stalwartly assisted with its production. Sue Mattson's editing further improved the work. Lael Morgan and Kent Sturgis offered many helpful suggestions.

To all I express my heartfelt thanks.

A word of appreciation must go also to the staffs of the Alaska rooms of Anchorage's Z. J. Loussac Library and the University of Alaska, Anchorage library and of the Alaska archives at the university's Elmer E. Rasmuson Library at Fairbanks; and to personnel of the legislative information office in Anchorage.

Introduction

MORE THAN HALF OF THEM ARE GONE NOW, the delegates to the Alaska Constitutional Convention, and the youngest of those surviving are in their sixties.

For most of the men and women who participated in that historic convention, the writing of the state constitution was one of the most satisfying experiences of their lives, and they would ever after take great pride in what they had accomplished. In the aftermath of the convention, the constitution was hailed nationally as a model document embodying the best features of the best state constitutions, and over the years since then it has proved to be a serviceable plan for government requiring relatively little amending.

The delegates went to Fairbanks with a sense of mission. First and foremost, they would be advancing the then-languishing statehood cause, showing the nation they were politically mature and fully capable of assuming the responsibilities of statehood. Second, they would have the opportunity to design a state government of, by and for Alaskans, a government with lines of accountability sharply drawn, the kind of government that had never existed in the Territory of Alaska. Closely watched by their fellow Alaskans, they knew the cause rode on how well they did their work.

Though they knew little about constitution-writing (constitution writers don't usually have prior experience), the delegates, most of them longtime Alaskans, brought to their task considerable common sense and a wealth of experience in public matters. Most of the fifty-five delegates had served in public office at some level. They had been mayors, councilmen, city and territorial officials, members of school boards and other local and territorial boards and commissions. Seventeen had seen service in territorial legislatures.

E. B. Collins, the oldest delegate, over eighty, had been speaker in the first territorial legislature in 1913; Mildred Hermann, director of the

Office of Price Administration for Alaska during World War II; Katherine Nordale, collector of customs for Alaska; Burke Riley, director of vocational rehabilitation for the Territory of Alaska, special assistant to Governor Ernest Gruening, and secretary of Alaska (essentially lieutenant governor). Ralph Rivers had been a territorial attorney general, B.D. Stewart a territorial commissioner of mines. M.J. (Mike) Walsh was a member of the University of Alaska's Board of Regents.

Four delegates—Mrs. Hermann, Frank Peratrovich, Victor Rivers, and Warren A. Taylor—were members of the Alaska Statehood Committee, created by the legislature in 1949 to work for statehood.

A wide range of occupations was represented at the convention. There were bush pilots, fishermen, miners, law enforcement officers, businessmen, engineers, clergymen. Thirteen delegates were attorneys. (See list of delegates in appendix.)

Eight delegates were born in Alaska, six in foreign countries and the remainder in the United States. Their ages ranged from twenty-nine to the early eighties with most from forty to sixty.

All but one, Nome pioneer Mike Walsh, were chosen in a special election on September 13, 1955. Howard Lyng of Nome had died following his election and Attorney General J. Gerald Williams reluctantly concluded that since Lyng had been unopposed in the election and there was therefore no runner-up, the governor should appoint as his successor the person who had received the greatest number of write-in votes in the district. That person was Walsh, who had recieved three.[1]

The special election was affected by one other development which if not for the timely amendment of federal law could have changed the course of Alaska's political history.

The Organic Act under which the Territory was governed provided that "no member of the legistlature shall hold...any office which has been created, or the salary...of which [has] been increased, while he was a member, during the term for which he was elected and for one year after the expiration of such a term..."[2] With this prohibition in mind, convention candidate Robert Kederick, reporter for the *Daily Alaska Empire* (and future associate editor of the *Anchorage Daily Times*), challenged the legality of the candidacy of Burke Riley, one of his opponents who had served in the 1955 legislature which had authorized and funded the election and convention. The case went before U.S. District Judge J. L. McCarrey Jr. in Anchorage who ruled in favor of Kederick.

The ruling would have ended candidacies of nine members of the 1955 lawmaking body, all Democrats, subsequently elected convention delegates. It was rendered meaningless by swift amendment of the Organic Act by a Democratic Congress. E. L. (Bob) Bartlett, Alaska's delegate in the House of Representatives, had requested this action, which cleared the way for any legislator to become a candidate for convention delegate.[3] Among the nine were William A. (Bill) Egan whose service as convention president led to his election as first governor of the future State of Alaska, and Ralph Rivers, the state's first congressman.

A special apportionment plan had been devised for election of convention delegates to ensure territory-wide representation, and the convention undoubtedly was the broadest-based group ever to assemble in Alaska to that time. Thirteen delegates were from Anchorage, the largest city, eleven from Fairbanks, seven from Juneau, and the remainder from eighteen other communities.

Six women participated in the convention. There was one Native delegate, Frank Peratrovich, a Tlingit Indian leader and veteran legislator, among the first Natives elected to the territorial lawmaking body.[4]

Although the election was nonpartisan, most of the delegates could be politically classified. A majority were Democrats.

Before the delegate election, some Alaskans feared the convention would be infiltrated by persons representing interests opposed to statehood. *Anchorage Daily Times* editor and publisher Robert B. Atwood, long an advocate of statehood, editorialized: "There is a strong possibility that the opposing forces [he mentioned the Seattle-based Alaska canned salmon industry] will seek representation on the floor of the convention through election of Trojan Horses who will represent special interest more effectively than the public interests of Alaska. . ."[5]

There was no need to worry. Most of the delegates, forty-seven of the fifty-five, were staunch statehood supporters, favoring Alaska's admission to the Union at the earliest possible time. Only one, avowedly, didn't want statehood, Nome gold dredge owner Peter L. Reader.[6]

The delegates would labor under some restraint at the convention. The constitution would have to include provisions usually required by statehood legislation, which meant generally that it was to be republican in form, make no distinction in civil or political rights on the basis of race or color, and be compatible with the U.S. Constitution and Declaration of Independence. The constitution was also to be submitted to Alaska voters for approval, which meant it would have to be a good one reflecting their hopes and expectations to the greatest possible degree. These requirements precluded a radical approach to constitution-making.

4 / Reaching for a Star

To succeed at their task, the delegates would have to exercise extraordinary discipline. Partisan politics and sectionalism could have no place at the convention. However hotly they might debate the issues, they would in the end have to stand together.

1
Getting Under Way

"THE HOUR APPOINTED by the Alaska Territorial Legislature having arrived for the convening of the Alaska Constitutional Convention, I do accordingly, as governor of this Territory, call the convention to order."

It was just after 10 a.m. on November 8, 1955, when Governor B. Frank Heintzleman brought down his gavel. Nearly a thousand heavily clothed people, undeterred by the fifteen-below-zero cold, had jammed into the steam-heated University of Alaska gymnasium (whose seating capacity was about 750) for the opening ceremonies of what would be the most important political event in the Territory's history to that time.

Fifty-three of the fifty-five convention delegates were there, seated in the front rows.[1] Frank Barr of Fairbanks was absent, downed by the flu. So was Frank Peratrovich whose thousand-mile flight to Fairbanks from Klawock in Southeastern Alaska had been disrupted by bad weather.

Among the dignitaries on the chrysanthemum-bedecked platform with Heintzleman were the foremost leaders of the statehood fight, former Territorial Governor Ernest Gruening and Delegate Bob Bartlett.

The gymnasium (later converted to a museum and now Signers Hall, home of the campus administration) was festooned with blue and gold bunting. The Stars and Stripes and Alaska's flag—the Big Dipper and North Star in gold on a deep-blue field—were brought forward by a color guard and placed on the platform. For the day, the building had been named Convention Hall.

Among the many news media representatives present for the opening ceremonies were Lawrence E. Davies, West Coast bureau chief for the *New York Times*, James Hutcheson of the Associated Press, and Florence Douthit of the *Fairbanks Daily News-Miner* who would be the only reporter to cover the convention continuously from beginning to end. Much of the newspaper's photo coverage of the convention was provided by Jim Douthit, her husband.

The governor called on the Reverend Roy Ahmoagak, Presbyterian minister from the Eskimo village of Wainwright, to give the invocation, then appointed John B. (Dixie) Hall, clerk of the U.S. District Court at Fairbanks, as temporary convention secretary. Following the first roll call, U.S. District Judge Vernon D. Forbes administered the oath of office to the delegates.

Heintzleman had words of advice the delegates had heard often in the weeks preceding the convention: Draft a flexible constitution that would permit Alaska to cope with "rapid and profound changes," a document providing for "a sound and uncomplicated" governmental structure and assuring "fundamental rights and liberties to all the people." Let the constitution be a statement of basic principles and leave lawmaking to legislators.[2]

Fairbanks Mayor Douglas Preston, Dr. Ernest N. Patty, president of the university, and Kenneth Carson, president of the student body, welcomed the delegates to Fairbanks and the campus. Said Patty: "We all say that this is a historic occasion, but we are probably too close to the drama to really appreciate how historic it is. . . . We are proud to have you here, and we are confident that when your final clause is written that your work will stand as one of the finest state constitutions."

In the election for temporary convention president, the delegates chose Mildred Hermann, a Juneau attorney who would shortly be characterized as the "undisputed queen mother of the convention" for her frequent goading of her fellow delegates to get on with decision-making. She was a large woman and often joked about her size. She had been a member of the Alaska Statehood Committee since its creation in 1949. She had reserved her room in Fairbanks' Nordale Hotel even before she knew she had been elected a convention delegate.[3]

Now, after she had accepted the gavel from Heintzleman, she quipped: "I suppose I should make a little 'bang' to express the symbol of my authority and my appreciation of the honor—as well as my wonder if it is a concession to a minority group."

Next the convention heard from Bob Bartlett, who had grown up in the Territory and worked as a newspaperman and gold miner. President Franklin D. Roosevelt had appointed him secretary of Alaska in 1939, an office he resigned from in 1944 to run for delegate. The popular Bartlett was now in his sixth term.

He told the delegates: "...here you are, each and every one of you, marked out by destiny not only to confront the judgment of your peers, your fellow Alaskans, but to have your names inscribed forever in Alaska history." Then he moved on to his theme: Alaska's vast store of natural resources must be safeguarded against the wrong kind of exploitation.

"Alaska's tradition of 'boom and bust' communities is due in no small measure to the hard, cold fact that mineral development was solely for the purpose of exploitation with no concern for permanent and legitimate growth. The decline of Alaska's once-great fisheries is traceable in great degree to this same attitude with its concept of ruthless plundering of a great natural resource without regard to the welfare of the mass of average citizens who make their living from the sea."

In establishing basic policy in the natural resources field, Bartlett said, the convention must aim to promote orderly development with "effective safeguards against the exploitation of the heritage by persons and corporations whose only aim is to skim the gravy and get out, leaving nothing that is permanent to the new state."

Ernest Gruening was given a standing ovation when he moved to the lectern to speak. Always outspoken, the former governor had his supporters and critics. Now he was enjoying a new popularity. He was to deliver a major address the next day, so on this first day of the convention he spoke briefly.

The convention's "greatest importance," Gruening said, "arises from the fact that it is the first occasion which is wholly of, for, and most important, by the people of Alaska. . . . Many things have been done for us; even more things have been done to us, but very little have we been permitted to do by us. . . .

"What a challenge then to create in these far-northern latitudes a shining and eternal example of what we want to call the American way of life, to make Alaska not merely a bulwark defense for the whole hemisphere, for the free world, but a spiritual citadel of the American idea. It can only be done by the application to Alaska of basic American principles, the most basic of which is government by consent of the governed..."

(There was more applause at the end but for Gruening the occasion could not have been what he had looked forward to: just before the convention opened he had learned that his 32-year-old son Peter, United Press manager in Australia, had committed suicide.[4])

Much of the groundwork for the convention had been laid by the Alaska Statehood Committee. Robert Atwood had been chairman of the committee since its creation in 1949. In his address, he told of the committee's pre-convention activities, chief of which was retaining the Public Administration Service of Chicago, a nationally recognized nonprofit organization, to prepare constitutional studies—studies of the governmental experiences of the forty-eight states—and provide consultant services to the convention.[5]

Each delegate would receive a three-volume set of these studies. In addition, Atwood said, information on the rules and organization of other conventions as well as a portfolio on Hawaii's constitutional convention experience would be made available. An extensive library of pertinent material had been assembled for delegate use.

The opening ceremonies were not without a few rough spots. Near the end, Mrs. Hermann was feeling her way. She wondered out loud if the benediction came before a motion to adjourn. "We still have some more music of course but I want to get organized so we do this right."

The program next called for the playing of "Alaska's Flag" by Miss Lorraine Donoghue on the James E. Barrack Memorial Carillon, located in a separate building, and Mrs. Hermann announced it. There was a moment of silence, then President Patty spoke up: "There has been a slight accident with the carillon, so we'll just have to skip that this morning."

The ceremonies ended a few minutes past noon with a benediction by Father George Boileau, S.J. Then the delegates grouped for photographers and after lunch met briefly to learn who would serve on a temporary rules committee and what bus service would be available to shuttle them to and from Fairbanks, four miles away, where most had found accommodations. Electric plug-ins for head-bolt heaters, essential in the extreme cold to keep engines warm, would be made available by the university to delegates using their own vehicles for transportation.

Closing this final meeting of the opening day, Mrs. Hermann told the delegates, "We will not be in this building tomorrow but in the other building where you had your luncheon today. So don't anybody come back over here expecting to find a setup for a meeting."

The "other building" was the new student union building which the university had rushed to completion for the convention, the building in which the delegates would spend seventy-three of the seventy-five days allotted for constitution-writing. At convention's end, the university's Board of Regents would name it Constitution Hall.

So the delegates had come together and would shortly begin work on a constitution for the future State of Alaska. That was the immediate task. The ultimate goal was statehood.

2
Why Statehood?

WHY WERE ALASKANS so caught up in the statehood movement? Why was statehood so important to them?

Basically, what they sought was an end of the nearly total domination of their lives by the federal government and the right to govern themselves.

Most residents of the Territory had come north from the contiguous United States where if something were not to their liking they could tell it to their congressmen and register their protests in the voting booth. In Alaska they found they could do neither. They could not vote for the president of their country and their only representation in Congress was a "delegate" who sat in the House of Representatives. He could and did speak out for them but had no vote in that body.

This situation was particularly galling to Alaskans because they were U.S. citizens and paid taxes and served in the armed forces just as their fellow citizens in the states. Without the leverage of a full-fledged congressional delegation, they would rarely receive their rightful share of appropriations from federal programs or have any real influence in the formulation and implementation of these programs in the Territory. There were minor vexations too, such as having to clear through U.S. Customs like foreign nationals when traveling to the United States, a situation which prompted Robert Atwood to suggest in his *Anchorage Daily Times* that local residents, when deplaning in the states, should display their Anchorage garbage dump permits to identify themselves and indicate their feeling for the discriminatory immigration regulations.

Alaska was a federal domain with a large, deeply rooted bureaucracy answerable only to faraway Washington and therefore not particularly sensitive to the needs of residents of the Territory. The secretary of interior, responsible for the nation's territories and other possessions, was the principal overseer of Alaska. Most of the federal agencies whose operations had the greatest impact on the Territory's economy—

including the Fish and Wildlife Service, Bureau of Land Management, Bureau of Indian Affairs, Bureau of Mines, the Alaska Road Commission and the Alaska Railroad—were within his department.

The federal government was the chief law enforcer and dispensed all justice above the municipal level in Alaska. Each of four judicial divisions was presided over by a U.S. district judge appointed by the president for a four-year term, who in turn appointed the lesser court officials. A U.S. district attorney and marshal, also presidential appointees, were assigned to each division. There were no territorial courts.

Hobbled by Bureaucracy

"...Having resided in a Federal area all of my lifetime, I am certainly aware that the vast majority of Federal officers are well intentioned. It has long been my feeling, though, that in the Federal government there is too long a chain of command. It is oftentimes years before an unsatisfactory Federal regulation that carries the force of law can be changed. Our experience has been that the Congress itself will act more quickly to remedy an inequity than will a regulatory agency of the Government. . . ."
—Alaska-Tennessee Plan "Senator" William A. Egan, testifying for statehood before the House Subcommittee on Territorial and Insular Affairs, March 14, 1957

This hybrid judicial system—operating under both federal and territorial law—was woefully inadequate and subject to abuse. Fortunately for Alaskans, the bench was occupied more often than not by persons of integrity. District judges were usually replaced following a change of national administrations. When there were vacancies on the bench, the backlog of civil cases grew heavier and persons charged with crimes could look for no early disposition of their cases.

The court officials with whom territorial residents were most familiar were the U.S. commissioners who presided over the lower courts and performed a host of other duties. They were legal jacks-of-all-trades, serving as magistrates, justices of the peace, notaries public, coroners. The greatest abuses and omissions in the administration of justice occurred at the level of the commissioners, most of whom were untrained in the law. They were allowed to retain fees collected as compensation for their services, but except in the large communities these fees were insufficient to support them and many had other occupations, which inevitably gave rise to conflicts of interest. And it must have occurred to some that it would be to their benefit to encourage fee-producing legal proceedings.

The U.S. Constitution gave Congress "the power to dispose of and make all needful rules and regulations respecting the territory...belonging to the United States..." Thus Alaskans had to look to Congress for most of their needs, and they could do for themselves only what Congress would allow them to do. The Territory had no inherent powers.

Alaska had had an appointed governor and court system since 1884 and a delegate to Congress since 1906. But it was not until 1912, forty-five years after its purchase from Russia, that Congress decided Alaskans were entitled to a degree of self-government. The Organic Act approved that year allowed them to establish a two-house legislature but narrowly limited what that body could do.

The Territory was effectively prohibited from managing the fish and game resources (commercial fishing was Alaska's principal industry), from constructing and maintaining roads, disposing of public lands, establishing counties. Neither the Territory nor municipalities could assume bonded indebtedness, and a ceiling was imposed on taxes they might levy. Such prohibitions insured that few public facilities would be constructed.

The Organic Act's concluding section probably best reflected Congress's attitude toward the Territory—and the influence of the absentee (nonresident) commercial interests in Alaskan affairs: "All laws passed by the legislature...shall be submitted to Congress by the president...and, if disapproved by Congress, they shall be null and of no effect."

Unable to make substantial capital improvements and offer land to prospective entrepreneurs, there was little the Territory could do to encourage development. Absentee interests—principally the canned salmon, shipping and large mining companies—could be counted on to try to block all attempts by the Territory and its municipalities to impose or increase taxes or to undertake new functions which might require raising additional revenue. The prohibition against establishing counties was recognized as a measure to keep at a minimum the cost of government—and of doing business—in Alaska.

Federal laws providing for the conveyance of public lands to the private sector for development were applicable to Alaska but had little beneficial effect because of the long-standing federal practice of withdrawing great tracts of land from public use, a practice which denied access to many of the more valuable resources of the Territory.

On the eve of statehood, the territorial government was still the monstrosity it had long been, comprising more than two dozen operating departments, offices, boards and commissions in the executive branch. The governor, secretary of Alaska and adjutant general were appointed by the president. Four department heads were elected, five were appointed by the governor, and the remaining agency heads were appointed by boards and commissions. And there were other boards and commissions with various functions.

The territorial legislatures over the years had created this multiplicity of semi-independent boards and commissions to withhold as much power as they could from the appointed governor and thereby exercise a degree of control over Alaskan affairs. The governor, as chief executive of the Territory, did appoint the members of most of these bodies but the appointments were subject to confirmation by the elected legislatures. The government resulting from this inherently abrasive relationship was one with authority so diffused it was virtually impossible to establish sound fiscal accountability and fix responsibility for many of its acts.

If there were one symbol of the economic discrimination Alaskans sought to end through statehood it was the salmon trap, a highly efficient means of catching fish controlled primarily by the big absentee canning interests. Twice they had voted overwhelmingly to eliminate traps, but the vote meant nothing, as the chief lobbyist for the canned salmon industry pointed out to a congressional subcommittee. "The referendum was held pursuant to an act of the legislature, and neither the legislature or the people of Alaska have any power to regulate or control the fisheries...It is similar to a straw vote or Gallup poll," said W. C. Arnold, a one-time U.S. commissioner in Alaska known throughout the Territory as Judge Arnold.[1]

Many Alaskans believed the fish traps were largely responsible for the decline of the salmon pack. Whatever the cause, the production curve dipped downward from the record pack of 8.5 million cases in 1936 to 3.6 million in 1952 to 1.8 million in 1959, the last year of federal management of the Alaska salmon resource.[2] The traps caught a large percentage of the salmon taken each year. As long as they had their traps, the canners were assured supplies of fish virtually on their own terms. They did not have to pay much attention to the price demands of Alaskan fishermen and they could—and at times did—refuse to buy their fish, or would buy only a portion of their catches. With the traps, often manned by nonresidents, what they had amounted to an exclusive right of fishery.

The big absentee companies, which often brought their own work forces to the Territory, could well afford to maintain lobbyists in the nation's capital to apprise lawmakers of the "needs" of Alaska. These interests helped themselves to the natural wealth of the Territory and left little behind to foster its development. In the long run, this narrow self-interest would become one of the most cogent arguments for statehood.

The conditions under which most Alaskans lived did not add up to some kind of gulag. Most had chosen to settle in the Territory and found a good life. But as Americans they were not willing to accept indefinitely their inferior political status.

Delegate Anthony J. (Tony) Dimond, who had long fought against the discriminations to which Alaskans were subjected, put it this way: "Unless we are willing to abandon our historic positions, we are bound to demand statehood at the earliest possible time. The whole form and fabric of our free government is based upon the assumption that people can govern themselves in better fashion than they can be governed by anyone else."[3]

3

The Fight for Statehood

A CAMPAIGN FOR STATEHOOD before the massive development and influx of people that came with World War II would have been unrealistic. Alaska's prewar resident population was small and scattered. There was neither a widespread clamor for statehood nor a consensus among Alaskans on the need of it. The heavy federal hand on the Territory, retarding its political and economic development, bothered many Alaskans but most believed that what was wrong could be made right eventually through the efforts of their delegate and legislative memorials—appeals—to the national administration and Congress. But after the war, with problems and needs rapidly mounting and the shortcomings of territorial status glaring, it became clear that nothing less than statehood would do.

There was nothing presumptuous about asking for admission to the Union. The Treaty of Cession conveying Alaska to the United States declared that residents "shall be admitted to the enjoyment of all the rights, advantages and immunities of citizens of the United States." And the U.S. Supreme Court would later hold that incorporated territories—Alaska was then such a territory—were destined to become states. Delegate James Wickersham introduced the first statehood bill in 1916; Delegate Anthony Dimond introduced a bill in 1943.

The statehood cause first gained national attention in 1946 when President Harry Truman in his State of the Union message urged Alaska's admission "as soon as it is certain that this is the desire of the people of that great Territory." The 1945 territorial legislature on the recommendation of Governor Ernest Gruening and Delegate Bob Bartlett, who had succeeded Dimond, had provided for such a referendum. In the 1946 general election Alaskans voted 9,630 to 6,822 for statehood. The Alaska Statehood Association, formed in advance of the election "to win the referendum vote," published and distributed throughout the Territory an informational booklet which drew heavily on Dimond's writings and speeches on behalf of statehood.[1] Gruening had suggested formation of such an association. Evangeline Atwood, wife of Robert Atwood, was a principal organizer.

The first of six memorials that would be presented to the president and Congress over the next dozen years asking for statehood was approved by the territorial legislature in 1945. But with basic territorial needs running far ahead of revenues, the memorial was somewhat premature in maintaining that Alaska had "fulfilled all of its obligations admirably and complies with all requisites of statehood."

Gruening had long exhorted the legislatures to overhaul the Alaska tax structure to capture a greater share of the resource-generated wealth that flowed out of the Territory each year. The few existing taxes were minimal. At war's end he resumed this appeal, pointing out that new people, many of them veterans, were coming to Alaska in large numbers, housing was scarce, tuberculosis rampant in the rural areas, more schools, water and sewer systems and other public facilities were needed, and a large budget deficit was in prospect. The 1947 legislature largely ignored his request.

The governor had aroused passions since his arrival in Alaska in 1939. Seen by some Alaskans as a carpetbagging politician from the East bent on making a new career for himself at their expense, they considered him presumptuous in telling them what they should do. Others saw him as a brilliant, dynamic leader who would promote development of the Territory and help them attain first-class citizenship. To the long-entrenched absentee commercial interests, who enjoyed a comfortable degree of influence among Alaska legislators, particularly senators, he was potentially a disturber of the status quo and therefore an enemy.

Inaction by the 1947 legislature brought on a financial crisis the following year. Its failure to enact new taxes, primarily an income tax on individuals and corporations, left the Territory unable to pay many of its bills. Only by obtaining private loans was it able to keep the University of Alaska open. The Territory was not totally without money. It had some special funds—funds dedicated to specific functions—but these could not be tapped to cover general operating expenses.

If the 1947 legislature was the worst legislature ever, as Gruening maintained, the 1949 body (legislatures met every other year) would be rated one of the best by him and many Alaskans. It quickly did what was required, and more. A net income and other taxes were enacted that returned the Territory to solvency and in the 1951-52 biennium would generate nearly three times the revenues of 1947-48.

Now statehood could be legitimately pursued, and to advance the cause the 1949 legislature created the bipartisan, nongovernmental Alaska Statehood Committee and appropriated $80,000 for its use. In so doing, the lawmakers officially made statehood a goal. The committee was to assemble materials and make studies and recommendations to assist the Territory in the "framing of a fundamentally sound and workable state constitution" and in dealing with "the many problems that will attend transition from territorial status to statehood..."

The eleven committee members were to be appointed by the governor and confirmed by the legislature. Delegate Bartlett, Anthony Dimond, and the territorial governor were to be ex officio members of the committee, which was to dissolve when a constitution was approved by the electorate. Gruening selected an outstanding committee that worked diligently throughout its life. Robert Atwood, Anchorage newspaper publisher and a Republican, was elected chairman, W. L. Baker, Ketchikan newspaper publisher, a Democrat, vice chairman, and Mildred Hermann, a Juneau attorney and a Republican, secretary.

Since 1947, when the House Subcommittee on Territorial and Insular Possessions had held the first hearings on statehood in Alaska, statehood legislation had been before the national lawmakers almost continuously, pressed on them doggedly by Bob Bartlett. In a special message to Congress in 1948, President Truman again urged that Alaska be made a state. He presented recommendations for dealing with a number of Alaska's problems and needs but emphasized that in the long run "the most important action the government can take...is to permit Alaska to become a state."

An Alaska statehood bill was passed by the House of Representatives early in 1950 but was not acted upon by the Senate. In June of that year, war broke out in Korea and there were matters more urgent than Alaska statehood to consider. The Territory's population in 1950—128,643—was nearly double that of 1939, and this new war would bring in many thousands more for the jobs created by another defense construction boom. The statehood movement grew with the population which reached an estimated 160,000, exclusive of military personnel, in 1952.

With the inauguration of Dwight Eisenhower in 1953, Alaskans for a brief moment felt that statehood was near at hand, for in 1950, when he was president of Columbia University, he had called for the quick admission of Alaska and Hawaii to the Union. But their hopes were soon dashed. In his first State of the Union message the president recommended the admission of Hawaii but made no mention of Alaska.

Alaskans, particularly members of the 1953 territorial legislature, most of them Republicans swept into office in the Eisenhower landslide, were shocked at this development. House members immediately sent off a telegram to the new president calling on him to "express your continued support for Alaska statehood at the earliest opportunity."[2] Eisenhower declined to accommodate them then and in his 1954 State of the Union message would ignore Alaska once more while calling again for Hawaiian statehood.

Delegate Bartlett, a Democrat, had also expressed his disappointment at the president's decision in 1953 to press only for Hawaiian statehood, saying that "for the first time in all the years Hawaii and Alaska have worked together, it [statehood] has been made a partisan issue."[3]

He had a point, and many others saw it that way. Hawaii had traditionally voted Republican and if made a state could be expected to send two Republicans to the U.S. Senate where the GOP held a one-seat edge. Though Republicans controlled the Alaska legislature in 1953, the Territory's delegate since 1932 had been a Democrat and the Democratic party there was still strong. It was just possible Alaska would send one or more Democrats to Washington, which would neutralize any Republican gains.

The Senate in 1954 combined a House-passed Hawaii statehood bill with its own Alaska bill, rejected attempts to make the territories commonwealths, and approved the legislation, but the House hadn't any intention of acting on it. "We have a pretty busy program and can't waste time with something that can't pass," said House Speaker Joe Martin. As far as he knew, the president hadn't changed his mind about wanting statehood conferred only on Hawaii.[4]

Ernest Gruening, ardent advocate of statehood, had stepped down as governor in 1953 and B. Frank Heintzleman, former regional forester for Alaska, was appointed by President Eisenhower to succeed him. Intense infighting for the governorship among prominent Alaska Republicans, including Walter J. Hickel, a future state governor, had led to the appointment of Heintzleman, who had not been caught up in the political donnybrook. Almost from the first, the new governor, who had lived in Juneau for many years, gained the enmity of party regulars in Anchorage who were at war with Southeastern Alaska Republicans for control of the party. And his subsequent stand for eventual rather than immediate statehood further alienated him from these and many other Alaskans.

Heintzleman brought down more criticism on himself in 1954 when he suggested in a letter to House Speaker Martin, made public following Senate passage of the combined Alaska-Hawaii bill, that Alaska be partitioned and a state made of the area comprising the southeastern, southcentral and interior regions—"that portion of the Territory that is developed, that embraces all the larger metropolitan centers and in which 85 percent of the population resides." Statehood supporters were appalled. Operation Statehood, a nonpartisan citizens' action group formed the prior year in Alaska, wired the governor: "Alaskans are shocked at your proposal to dismember Alaska and divorce the state from its resources. All Alaskans are entitled to statehood..."[5] The proposed state would have been separated from many of Alaska's resource-rich areas (including the North Slope where one day the nation's largest oil field would be discovered). Many feared Heintzleman's proposal would jeopardize the statehood drive, but it had no great effect in Washington.

There was one development in 1954 which dramatized and strengthened the statehood cause: the publication of Ernest Gruening's *The State of Alaska*. Since stepping down as governor the year before, after more than thirteen years in office, Gruening had devoted himself to completing this history of Alaska, which contained compelling arguments for statehood. It became a national bestseller.

The Case for Statehood

"...(T)he book presents a powerful argument for statehood. Undoubtedly, it was written with that purpose in view. The case it makes is all the more compelling because it is predicated not upon an emotional plea by one whose emotions are so surely involved, but rather upon a relentless review of facts which expose with dramatic clarity the disheartening effect of governmental neglect, confusion and bureaucracy on the one hand and exploitation by powerful economic interests. . . ."

—Review of *The State of Alaska*, in *Saturday Review*, February 12, 1955

But Eisenhower still held to his Hawaii-only position. He told a press conference early in 1955 that he favored Alaska statehood in principle but would have to oppose it because of national security considerations. He did not elaborate.[6]

Several days later, Senator Henry Jackson, chairman of the Senate Subcommittee on Territories and Insular Affairs, wrote the president to ask "why continuation of the 80-year-old inferior political status of the Territory is desirable for security reasons." His subcommittee stood ready, he wrote, wanting only "a clear statement as to the type of statehood legislation that would be acceptable to your administration."[7]

Eisenhower responded vaguely, suggesting that statehood could impair the military's freedom of movement and action in strategically important Alaska at a critical time in world affairs. Unless Congress could come up with a formula that would ensure the military such freedom, he felt it would be "imprudent" to make Alaska a state. In any case, he added, "I am in doubt that any form of legislation can wholly remove my apprehension about granting statehood immediately."[8]

The national lawmakers were also reluctant to do much about statehood in 1955. After an acrimonious, low-swinging debate in the House in May on a combined Alaska-Hawaii bill, the measure was sent back to committee. During the debate, which came just a year after the Army-McCarthy hearings, one vociferous opponent charged that statehood would deliver the Hawaiian state government to the Communist party. Southern Democrats worried that their states' rights (anti-civil rights) voting bloc would be severely weakened and conservative Republicans that their states would lose seats in the House if two new states were created.

In reporting that House action, *Time* magazine commented that prospects for statehood for either territory "are dim for the foreseeable future; the steam has gone out of the statehood movement."[9]

At this low point in the statehood campaign, Alaskans were preparing to elect delegates to a convention to draft a state constitution. They didn't have to do that. Most statehood bills that had come before Congress authorized the writing of a constitution after passage of the legislation.

Hawaii, however, had had a constitution since 1950 and it was now, in 1955, being cited as evidence of that territory's readiness to become a state. Testifying in favor of Hawaiian statehood, Interior Secretary Douglas McKay told the House Committee on Interior and Insular Affairs on February 4: "Recently the people of Hawaii have given further proof of their skill in political affairs by drafting and adopting a constitution for the proposed new state that reflects high qualities of statesmanship."

So Alaskans were pressing ahead with their plan to hold a constitutional convention. There was nothing to lose.

4

Organizing the Convention

THE ALL-IMPORTANT TASK of electing the president would be the first order of business on the second day of the Alaska Constitutional Convention—after the delegates had heard from Ernest Gruening.

The Alaska Statehood Committee had brought him to Fairbanks to deliver a keynote address to the convention. "He will have a message that we hope will be heard around the world," Robert Atwood told the delegates at the opening ceremonies. "We know it will be an enduring document in the statehood movement.[1] We trust it will be inspiring and informative for you."

The erudite Gruening had graduated from Harvard with a medical degree but made journalism his career. He had edited New York and other East Coast newspapers and been managing editor of *The Nation* magazine before his appointment as director of the Interior Department's Division of Territories and Island Possessions and then governor of Alaska.

In his address he focused and enlarged on the theme that existing political and economic discriminations against Alaskans amounted to nothing less than colonialism—and nothing less than statehood would put an end to this condition, so alien to American ideals and goals in the modern world.

"We Alaskans believe—passionately—that American citizenship is the most precious possession in the world," he said. "Hence, we want it in full measure; full citizenship instead of half-citizenship; first-class instead of second-class citizenship. We demand equality with all other Americans, and the liberties, long denied us, that go with it."

Only statehood would bring this equality and Alaskans must be unrelenting in their efforts to achieve it, he concluded:

"We are agreed that there is only one form of self-government that is possible for Alaska. And so we are drawing up the constitution for the state that we fervently hope will soon come to be...

"This constitutional convention is an important mobilization. But the battle still lies ahead, and it will require all our fortitude, audacity, resoluteness—and maybe something more—to achieve victory. When the need for that something more comes, if we have the courage—the guts—to do whatever is necessary, we shall not fail. That the victory will be the nation's as well as Alaska's—and the world's—should deepen our determination to end American colonialism."

As the former governor concluded, the delegates gave him another standing ovation. Then, the ceremonies and speeches at an end, they turned to the business of electing their permanent officers.

There were four nominees for convention president—E. B. Collins, Victor Rivers, his brother Ralph Rivers, and William Egan. John H. Rosswog of Cordova put forward Egan's name, telling his fellow delegates he felt him well qualified because of his long residence in the Territory "and his experience with Mason's [manual of legislative rules and procedures]."

Egan, who had just turned forty-one, was born in Valdez and still lived there. As a freshman legislator in 1941 he had cosponsored the first bill to call for a referendum on statehood. The measure cleared the House but failed in the Senate. He served in six other legislatures—in both the lower and upper chambers—and was House speaker in 1951.

Egan led the others on the first two ballots and won the required majority of votes, twenty-eight, on the third. Only Victor Rivers, fifty, a civil engineer from Anchorage and also a veteran legislator, mounted a challenge but this faded away on the final ballot as delegates switched to Egan.

Bluff and outspoken, Rivers was the only delegate to actively seek the convention presidency.[2] In nominating him, Steve McCutcheon credited Rivers with being the driving force behind the 1949 legislature's enactment of new tax measures which put the Territory on a sound financial basis.

Egan had hitched a ride up to Fairbanks with a trucker. Delegates Burke Riley and George McLaughlin hailed him when he jumped down from the truck cab on a downtown street and urged him to run for president. They and other delegates saw him as the ideal person to serve as presiding officer and they told him so. Egan backed away from the idea then but was soon persuaded to become a candidate.[3]

It has been speculated that the forceful, cigar-smoking Rivers might have won had the contest taken place in the legislative arena but that the soft-spoken Egan had greater appeal because he was less the prodding politician and more the type of person who would preside in an even-handed and impartial way.[4]

Handing over the gavel to Egan, Mildred Hermann offered her

congratulations and some cautionary words: "I commend you to act with dignity and humility."

Egan pledged he would "at all times strive to carry out the responsibilities that go with this office with dignity and fairness, [as] your temporary chairman has done."

Edward Davis of Anchorage called on the convention to give Mrs. Hermann a vote of thanks for her service, Mike Walsh moved to make it a rising vote of thanks, and the body unanimously concurred and rose to its feet to applaud.

Frank Peratrovich had not yet reached Fairbanks but the convention nonetheless made him first vice president. Ralph Rivers was elected second vice president. In nominating Peratrovich, George Sundborg said he should be given "a position of high rank in the convention because he is...a representative of the Indian people who lived here long before any of the rest of us came on the scene."

Thomas B. Stewart of Juneau, who had done more than anyone to make the convention a reality, was unanimously elected convention secretary. He had done much of the research for a convention call and chaired the 1955 legislature's Joint Committee on Statehood and Federal Legislation, the body which had drafted the convention enabling act. And as executive secretary of the Alaska Statehood Committee he had made most of the arrangements for the convention. He was not a delegate but his father, B. D. Stewart, sat in the convention.

John B. (Dixie) Hall also got a rising vote of thanks when he stepped down as temporary secretary, and he responded: "I will tell Judge Forbes what a rousing cheer we got when I got relieved...I am glad I met all of you. I'm not running for any office but if I do don't you all forget me." (He did run for office in 1962 and served two terms in the State Senate.)

Katherine Alexander (later Hurley), longtime executive secretary to Governor Gruening and now secretary of the territorial Senate, was appointed chief clerk of the convention. She had assisted Stewart in making preparations for the convention. Doris Ann Bartlett, daughter of Bob Bartlett, would serve with her on the convention staff.

The 1955 legislature appropriated $300,000 to cover the costs of the convention, the special delegate election and the future election in which Alaskans would render a decision on the constitution about to be drafted. The delegates were to be reimbursed for their travel costs and receive per diem of twenty dollars a day and fifteen dollars for each day of service at the convention.

The snow-covered university campus, on high ground overlooking the broad Tanana Valley and the Alaska Range, from which Mount McKinley stood out on clear days, was already proving to be a good location for the convention. The delegates had been warmly welcomed to the campus but were being left alone as they got down to business. Few lobbyists for special interests would be on hand during the convention to give advice, not so much because the campus was remote from the rest of Alaska but because the prospects for statehood were then bleak. In such an environment, the delegates could indulge their idealism.

Juneau, the territorial capital, had been considered but rejected as a convention site. The town could have provided all the necessary accommodations but it "had the unsavory reputation that too often goes with legislative politics: special interest lobbying, heavy drinking, and the like."[5]

The first days of the convention were given over to settling into Constitution Hall, adopting rules, organizing committees, developing a budget, hiring employees, ordering supplies and equipment, arranging for the recording of plenary sessions. There were hundreds of details, large and small, to be attended to.

E. B. Collins had a problem: "Mr. President, it is a matter of small importance but it seems that each night our different chairs have been scrambled and it is a hard matter in the morning to find my location. I hesitate to take my jackknife and cut my initials on these chairs. I think something might be done to prohibit changing of the seats." The matter was resolved when tables and chairs replaced the student chair-desks and each delegate was assigned a specific place.

A little confusion arose over names at first: there were two Fischers, Victor and Helen (unrelated), two named Rivers, a Sundborg and Londborg, and a Hilscher and Kilcher. When it came to seating, George Sundborg couldn't help observing that "one of the Fischers had ended up stranded between two Rivers."

In the beginning too there was a heavy schedule of social activities. The delegates were guests of honor at public receptions and in private homes. They met members of the Fairbanks Chamber of Commerce, city officials, air base officers and university deans and department heads at a reception in President Ernest Patty's campus home. They were invited to attend the dedication of the $2.5 million Austin E. Lathrop High School (named for "Cap" Lathrop, Alaska's first industrialist, who had been ardently opposed to statehood).

The delegates watched a fighter scramble at Ladd Air Force Base (now Fort Wainwright) and were guests at a special dinner hosted by Lieutenant General Joseph H. Atkinson, head of the joint Alaskan Command. In remarks to his guests, the general pointed out there were 80,000 servicemen and dependents in the Territory. He hoped, he said, that the delegates would not write into the constitution anything that would hamper military operations or work undue hardship on military personnel. He emphasized he was asking no special privileges.⁶

On the fifth day, Frank Peratrovich made it into Fairbanks, and by the end of the first week the delegates were getting used to one another and some of the committees were scheduling meetings.

Observed the *Fairbanks Daily News-Miner*: "Now that the constitutional convention has been in session a week, we would like to comment on the earnestness and the capability of the delegates. . . . Usual political considerations that predominate political conventions and legislative sessions are entirely absent from the current convention, so far as we can see. For instance, William A. Egan...reports that not one delegate has come to him with a request to head a certain committee. All delegates stand willing to accept whatever task is given them and they are not inserting any of their ambitions or political beliefs in the proceedings."⁷

Egan commented that there was "some strain noticeable the first few days but I don't see it now. It's wonderful and maybe a miracle to see how these fifty-five people have left politics out of this convention. . . . My hope is that there won't be too many allusions to the way things are done in the legislature. This gathering is a new and different thing. With good faith already obvious here, the delegates don't need a legislative background."⁸

He had one other comment: He had decided to give up politics so he would have more time to devote to his family and business. He and his wife Neva had an eight-year-old son, Dennis, and operated the Valdez Supply Company, selling meats and groceries. When he attended legislative sessions she had to run the store alone, which was difficult.⁹ "But before I quit," Egan said, "I wanted to see the constitution shaped."

5
Open or Closed Committee Meetings?

THE CONVENTION had scarcely got under way when it ran aground on the question of whether or not its committee meetings would be open to the public.

The Rules Committee initially proposed closed meetings with the committees having the option of inviting the public if they so desired. The public would be notified of the time and place of meetings.

John Hellenthal of Anchorage, an attorney whose father had been a federal judge for the Territory, immediately objected to adopting the proposed rule when it came before the convention. If this rule were adopted "we would put ourselves open to the well-deserved criticism that we are meeting in secret session, which has an ugly connotation." He suggested that committees meet in public view, and if sensitive matters came up, such as the need to discuss personalities or decorum of the convention, these could be considered in executive session, which could be convened by a majority or two-thirds vote. This is the normal, typical rule in Congress and elsewhere, he said.

"Now if the occasion develops that crackpots or someone...start plaguing us, then we can take a prophylactic rule such as the one recommended here..." Hellenthal, who had been Anchorage city attorney, continued. "I have been through this before with city councils where they elected to meet 'secretly,' the word the newspapers always use, and I tell you that it does not work...If the need arises then let's handle the problem, but not now."

Victor Fischer, professional planning consultant from Anchorage and vice president of Operation Statehood, supported Hellenthal's stand, saying the convention was "being held in behalf of all the people of Alaska. . . . I think it is our responsibility to the public to give them an opportunity to watch this convention at work."

But all other speakers vigorously endorsed the proposed rule.

Ralph Rivers didn't want the public present "while we try to develop a consensus of our thinking during all of our exploratory work. We think the committee can do better work if the public is there on invitation."

Congressional committees and those of the Alaska legislature are open to the public only by invitation, argued George Sundborg, editor of the *Juneau Independent*. The Federal Constitutional Convention was totally closed and delegates were prohibited from discussing their work in public "and they came out with a pretty good result." He was confident that if public input were required at some point, the public would be admitted to committee meetings of the present convention, and that committees would admit a member of the public who made "a reasonable request" to attend meetings.

Mildred Hermann pointed out that the public could attend all meetings of the full convention, where the final work would be done. There was no need to open committee meetings. "It is just a matter of operating a little more efficiently and not burdening the public ear with some of the trivia that often comes up in committee meetings." She was sure committees would hold public hearings on matters of particular interest to the public. And, she concluded, the committee rooms were small, "just about big enough for the committees themselves, and when I get in one they're a little crowded."

Longtime legislator Warren Taylor of Fairbanks felt it wouldn't be in "the best interests of committees doing efficient work to allow the public to indiscriminately come into these little committee rooms, take up your time, distract your thoughts from matters of great importance." He believed committees would open their doors to persons who asked to attend meetings to speak on particular subjects.

During a recess, concerned delegates got together and discussed the situation, and when the convention came back to order Fischer offered a new rule which provided that committee meetings would be open to the public "at such times as may be designated by the respective committees," and if a committee "finds it to be in the public interest, upon application any citizen may attend committee sessions." The public was to be notified of the time and place of meetings.

Under this rule, Fischer explained, the committees would be "free to act as they feel will promote the work of their particular committee. In some cases they may feel that the committee sessions should be closed, but we certainly hope that in most cases unless they are just trying to work out ideas and talking very informally that the meetings will be open, but even if there is a closed meeting, under the second sentence, upon application the committee could still open their sessions up to specific individuals."

The rule was adopted—and news media representatives immediately voiced strong protest, which could have come as no surprise to

Hellenthal. In a long editorial, the *Fairbanks Daily News-Miner* sympathized with the delegates' desire to operate "without undue lobbying and interference from...the general public," but wasn't "exactly pleased with the manner in which convention delegates have shut off public attendance at committee meetings."[1] The editorial went on:

> ...This constitution is the property of the people of Alaska and we feel they have a right to know how it is being drafted. Yesterday the delegates voted to require any person who wishes to attend a committee meeting to seek permission from that committee at every meeting before this person can enter the meeting room. . . . As things stand now, our reporters...will be forced to devote a large portion of their time to the task of seeking permission to attend committee meetings. Since most of the work of the convention...will be accomplished at the committee meetings, the new rule, in effect, clamps what amounts to a press censorship on the...proceedings. Frankly, WE PROTEST. . . . It should certainly be possible to keep spectators under control by imposing a 'no speaking' rule....We... who are charged with 'covering' this event for virtually all of the newspapers and radio stations in Alaska are wondering how we will be able to accomplish our task in the face of the obstacles this new rule imposes. We are very disappointed with the attitude of the delegates on this matter. In our opinion, they have opened a great exercise in Democracy with a very undemocratic act.

The next day, a Saturday, the convention's Rules Committee, troubled by press reaction, quickly called in news media representatives to discuss the matter. At the "very calm, level-headed meeting, both sides aired their opinions, and an agreement was quickly reached that was satisfactory to all present," reported the *News-Miner*.[2]

On Monday, convention rules were formally adopted. The controversial rule regarding committee meetings had been replaced by a brief, somewhat ambiguous one: the public was to be notified of the time and place of meetings and "all committee *hearings* [hearings, not meetings] shall be public."

The adopted rule "skirts the issue of public meetings and apparently leaves it open to interpretation," commented the *News-Miner*.[3] But there was that "satisfactory" agreement with the media, and the Associated Press reported that the "interpretation given by Burke Riley, chairman of the Rules Committee, was that the meetings would be considered to be open."[4]

In its "On the Inside" column a week later, the *News-Miner* had this to say about the situation: "The aftermath of that controversy over

28 / Reaching for a Star

whether or not the press and public should be admitted to all sessions at the constitutional convention is unspectacular. The delegates quietly agreed to let the press sit in on any session it chose, although each committee sets its own policies about direct quotations and off-the-record remarks."[5]

And that's the way it would be. Throughout the convention the press had access to all meetings.

6

A One- or Two-House Legislature?

IN THE BEGINNING, the delegates spent most of their time in committee—doing research and conferring with consultants. There was little for them to do as a whole, in plenary session. In late November, not yet feeling the pressure of their deadline, they were still sorting things out, feeling their way.

Delegate Yule Kilcher, a Homer homesteader who had migrated to Alaska from Switzerland, thought Mount McKinley was an inappropriate name for North America's highest mountain and introduced a resolution proposing that it be renamed Denali, "the beautiful, ancient name" of the mountain. He withdrew his resolution after the committee to which it had been referred concluded it had no constitutional or legislative relevance.

Then there was the question of whether the daily prayers should be published in the convention journal. That came up when Maurice T. Johnson, a Fairbanks attorney and former legislator, moved that a prayer given by the Reverend Maynard D. Londborg be placed in the journal. Londborg was a delegate from Unalakleet where he served as a missionary for the Covenant Church of America. A number of suggestions were made before the matter was laid to rest: Put this one in but then skip it from now on. . . . Publish all the prayers every day; it wouldn't be fair to publish just one. . . . Publish just those of seventy-five words or less. . . . The delegates hear the prayers each day and receive guidance from them, so there's no need to publish them, which would only make more work for a hard-working staff.

If it's to be done, make it retroactive and include all of the prayers that have been given, said Mildred Hermann. "I very much want that one...[from] the man who said he hoped 'we would have no cobwebs in our brain and no lead in our feet.' "

In the end, the prayers would be left out of the journal (but they would be retained for posterity, in the minutes of the daily proceedings, produced from convention tapes).

President Egan with the assistance of an Advisory Committee on Committees had appointed fourteen standing committees to do the convention work. Eleven would be directly involved in drafting the various articles of the constitution. The other three would be concerned with rules, convention administration, and the style and wording of the finished articles (to make sure they were in proper form and read well).

Generally, upon introduction, proposed articles were read in full and the chairmen of committees which had prepared them would explain the articles and answer questions concerning them. The amending of articles, usually an extensive process including recesses for consultations among delegates, took place during a second reading. When in final form, including any amendments, the articles were brought back for a third reading and final consideration.

The first major debate of the convention took place at the end of November. At an evening session, to which the public was invited, the body resolved itself into a committee of the whole to decide whether the future state legislature should be a one-house (unicameral) or two-house [bicameral] assembly. The Committee on Legislative Branch, chaired by Anchorage photographer Steve McCutcheon, a former legislator, had asked the convention (itself an exercise in unicameralism) to do this so it would not waste time drafting a proposal that might be unacceptable from the start. It was a pivotal question. Other committees, in order to do their work, also needed to know what type of legislature the convention proposed to adopt.[1]

Heed The People

"I have seen no demand or, for that matter, no request from the people of Alaska that we depart from that (bicameral) system, and I doubt seriously that were we to experiment with a one-house system that the people would be pleased."
—Edward V. Davis

There was more to this matter than just the physical form of the legislature. A number of rural area delegates favored a bicameral body because one house likely would be apportioned on the basis of area rather than population, assuring significant bush representation. A unicameral body, they had no doubt, would be apportioned on the basis of population and consequently be topheavy with representatives of urban areas. The nation was still many years away from the Supreme Court's historic "one man, one vote" decision which would require that both houses of a bicameral state legislature be apportioned on the basis of population.[2]

In the debate, John A. McNees, Nome beverage company owner, presented the case for unicameralism. There would be adequate checks against possible excesses and abuses by such a body, he argued. Laws it might pass would be subject to veto by the governor; they could be set aside by the courts if unconstitutional and could be nullified by the people by referendum. A one-house legislature would take a closer look at legislation, and it would be more efficient and economical. With only one house to watch over, the news media could do a better job of informing the public of legislative actions.

Membership in a unicameral legislature, McNees went on, "carries greater prestige, dignity and greater opportunity for public service...and hence attracts more distinguished, outstanding and representative citizens. . . . The jealousy, friction and rivalry in the two houses is gone. Responsibility can be definitely fixed. . . . The single house permits closer and more effective relationships between the governor and executive departments and the legislature. . . . [It] does away with the need for conference committees."

A bicameral system, in which two bodies do the same work, is "unreasonable, illogical and required by no other government agency," said McNees, who had seen no service in the legislature.

Maurice Johnson countered that the courts could set aside illegal legislative acts but not unwise ones, and governors' vetoes could be overridden by lawmakers. And, he said, "if this bicameral system is such an illogical procedure, then the United States of America acting under that system...could never have reached its present position of economic, political and military strength."

"The ideal system for a legislature is the unicameral...and that is just exactly what is wrong with it," said Fairbanks bush pilot and legislator Frank Barr. "It is an ideal. It is backed by theorists who have never had any experience in the practical applications of their theories." As to shortcomings of such a system, he said lobbyists might find it far easier to control than a two-house legislature.

Others speakers argued that two houses afforded greater safeguards. The Senate tends to "cool off...a hot, impetuous" House, said Fairbanks attorney and legislator Robert J. McNealy. The two-house system was more likely "to hold in check any ill-advised or unwanted legislation," said George D. Cooper, owner of a Fairbanks ready-mixed concrete plant. Such a system gives lawmakers time to reconsider their actions, said E. B. Collins.

The state constitution they were about to draft "will correct any error that has been perpetrated...under our territorial form of government," said the Reverend R. Rolland Armstrong of Juneau, an administrator for the Presbyterian Board of National Missions, in voicing support for the bicameral system.

Anchorage attorney Edward V. Davis didn't think the convention should be considering anything but the traditional two-house legislature. He said he had "seen no demand or, for that matter, no request from the people of Alaska that we depart from that system, and I doubt seriously that were we to experiment with a one-house system that the people would be pleased."

Another Anchorage attorney, Seaborn J. Buckalew, thought the convention would "be taking the voters of Alaska by surprise" if it adopted a unicameral system. Ratification of the constitution would be put in doubt. But he found unicameralism attractive. "If it was not for the fact that we hadn't put this idea to the people beforehand, I would vote for a unicameral house."

Two houses are needed, said Victor Rivers, "in order to get a proper voice from the people in the more remote areas."

William Egan was one of the speakers endorsing bicameralism on the ground it was traditional and had served the nation well. "We know that our United States has become the freest, the fairest and the greatest nation on earth under the bicameral system, and I hope this convention will continue that form of legislative government," declared Egan, who had relinquished the chair to Burke Riley to take part in the debate, something he would not do often in the days ahead.

All states but Nebraska had bicameral legislatures and seemed to like that system, said Thomas C. Harris, an electronics engineer and hotel manager from Valdez. "So since we have got something that we know has worked pretty good, I can't see much use in changing it."

Other delegates besides Buckalew worried that adopting a unicameral system would imperil ratification of the constitution. John M. Cross, a pioneer military and commercial aviator from Kotzebue, was confident Alaska could successfully implement a unicameral or bicameral legislature but doubted "very much that we could sell [a constitution] with any but a two-house legislature."

"The most important consideration," said Dora Sweeney of Juneau, a former Senate secretary and currently a legislator, was to draft a constitution acceptable to Alaskans and Congress, and providing for a one-house legislature could thwart that objective. "I feel very strongly about this, that we must have the constitution so good and so easy to get an approval on...that it will go through."

Some of the delegates had talked about voting on the bicameral/unicameral question at the conclusion of the debate, but such a vote was never taken. There was no need for one. An overwhelming number of delegates favored the two-house legislature. Only Jack Hinckel, a petroleum products distributor from Kodiak, stood unequivocally for unicameralism with McNees.

Asked if a constitutional amendment providing for a unicameral legislature should be placed on the next general election ballot for their consideration, voters in the 1976 general election said yes, 58,782 to 55,204. The next legislature declined to take the action required to place such an amendment before the voters.

7

A New Capital?

THE ANTICIPATED BATTLE over location of the state capital—the only issue that would divide delegates along sectional lines—broke out early at the convention. At the end of the second week, Thomas Harris and Chris Poulsen, an Anchorage theater owner, submitted proposals that would have the voters determine where the capital should be established. Longtime Juneau lawyer R. E. Robertson shortly proposed that his hometown—where the territorial capital was located—be designated the state capital.

Here was a perilous moment, as the *Fairbanks Daily News-Miner* noted editorially: "As everyone in Alaska knows, mere mention of the possibility of changing the capital...brings a tremendous reaction from Southeastern Alaska. Juneau will fight tooth and nail to keep the capital, and we don't blame the residents of that city for their attitude. . . . All we have to say is, we hope the convention doesn't get snagged on this matter. . . . We certainly hope such an explosive issue isn't allowed to snarl the deliberations."[1]

The issue flared briefly on the thirty-first day. Harris, still firmly convinced that Juneau—in the southeastern panhandle, reachable only by boat or plane—was no place for the state capital, introduced a resolution providing that the constitution say nothing about capital location. The convention had, by resolution, stated its intent to draft a document embodying only fundamental governmental principles and a framework for state government, and the location of the capital, Harris maintained, would be out of place in such a document.

Objecting to the resolution, Maynard Londborg said the constitution had to designate a capital or there would be no official place of government if statehood were granted. Barrie White, an Anchorage newspaper dealer and former president of Operation Statehood, proposed amending the Harris resolution to provide a method for choosing a capital, without naming a site, to meet Londborg's objection.

But the convention wasn't ready yet to resolve this problem and it approved by voice vote a Robertson motion, seconded by Mildred Hermann, to table the resolution.

A week later, the Committee on Resolutions and Recommendations, after having considered all of the various capital proposals, came up with one of its own: that the convention adopt an ordinance (defined as temporary legislation not part of the constitution) that would place the state capital temporarily at Juneau and ten years after the constitution had gone into effect have the voters select a site from among several recommended by the legislature.

The Crux of the Matter

"There is little if any opposition to Juneau being the capital, but there seems to be a feeling among most of the delegates that the people of their areas would like a chance to vote on it."
—R. E. Robertson

Responsibility for drafting the final proposal on this matter lay with members of the Committee on Ordinances and Transitional Measures and after they had considered all others could agree only that for the time being the capital should remain at Juneau where the federal Organic Act of 1912 had placed it.

The committee proposal, Section 20 of the Schedule of Transitional Measures, "was the nearest thing that we could arrive at to get any degree of unanimity," said chairman Robert McNealy. It was a concession to "the property owners and others in Juneau and in the southeastern area." Among the nine committee members were William W. Knight and B. D. Stewart of Sitka and H. R. VanderLeest of Juneau, who liked the capital where it was.

Because it was part of the Schedule of Transitional Measures, Section 20 would not be a permanent part of the constitution and was included only to provide for an orderly transition to statehood, McNealy assured the delegates. Once Alaska was a state, a capital move could be undertaken by the legislature or by initiative, he said.

In the concluding debate on this crucial issue, James Hurley of Palmer, general manager of the Alaska Rural Rehabilitation Corporation, moved that "Palmer" be substituted for "Juneau" in Section 20, saying the Matanuska Valley farming community was centrally located and could be easily reached. Fairbanks lawyer Warren Taylor, who had long served in the legislature, offered an amendment to Hurley's amendment establishing the capital at Palmer "whenever...[it]

shall be able to provide a capitol building and other facilities comparable with the facilities and buildings available at Juneau." Over Taylor's objection, William Egan ruled his amendment out of order, calling it "facetious...not germane to the question." It didn't really matter. Hurley's amendment was not adopted.

The key vote in the capital debate came on a motion by John McNees to strike Section 20 from the Schedule of Transitional Measures. He favored keeping the capital at Juneau, for economic reasons, but didn't think the convention should tie itself "to definitely retaining it as a part of the constitution."

Victor Rivers, adamantly opposed to making Juneau the permanent capital, thought that "eventually the location of the capital should be left to the majority vote of the people after a reasonable interim for studies."

Speaking in support of the McNees amendment, Victor Fischer said he had "very grave doubts as to whether we could change the capital if it's provided in here as currently proposed...unless we have a qualification ...'until otherwise provided by law' [by the legislature] or 'until otherwise provided by a vote of the people'...We have no right to tie ourselves down and freeze the location in one particular place...because there are cost factors involved."

Seaborn Buckalew feared the proposed section "would permanently fix the capital at Juneau" and suggested it would be "safer and wiser to...insert such language as suggested by Mr. Fischer." A court challenge of the section, he said, might involve a judge from Juneau who "might find more strength in the decision...that this would be a permanent provision."[2]

The proposed section designating Juneau the capital should be retained, said McNealy, so the first state legislature "will at least know where...to meet." And, he reiterated, the Schedule of Transitional Measures was just a temporary part of the constitution.

McNees's amendment was rejected. So also was Yule Kilcher's, providing that Juneau would be the capital "unless decided otherwise by law." Ralph Rivers, in agreement with his brother, proposed an amendment that would make Juneau the capital but require the legislature to create—within five years after Alaska's admission to the Union—a capital site survey commission which would recommend a number of sites for a new capital. The voters would make the final selection. This amendment too was rejected.

R. E. Robertson had sized up his fellow delegates on this issue and when he returned home for Christmas told Juneauites the capital was safe until a referendum was held on the question of relocation. "There is little if any opposition to Juneau being the capital," he said at a public meeting. "But there seems to be a feeling among most of the delegates that the people of their areas would like a chance to vote on it."³

At the same meeting, Robert Boochever, president of the Juneau Chamber of Commerce (and a future justice of the Alaska Supreme Court and member of the U.S. Ninth Circuit Court of Appeals), said that if a provision designating Juneau the capital of the future state could not be placed in the constitution, there should be no mention of the capital at all. A referendum provision, he said, would cast doubt on the city's future and discourage investment there.

Section 20 was made part of the constitution. The convention didn't "get snagged" on the capital location question.

But in future years the state would be confronted time and again with this divisive issue.

There were several attempts to move the capital by initiative after Alaska became a state. The first, in the 1960 primary election, failed 18,865 to 23,972; the second, in the 1962 general election, was defeated 26,542 to 32,325. In the 1974 primary election, Alaskans voted 46,659 to 35,683 to relocate the capital. This successful initiative provided for appointment of a capital site selection committee which was to select three potential capital sites in the southcentral/interior region, none of which could be within thirty miles of Anchorage or Fairbanks. The voters were to make the final site selection. In the 1976 general election they chose Willow but in the 1978 general election turned down—88,783 to 31,491—a $966 million bond issue to build the new capital. The issue remained alive on the basis of the 1974 relocation vote and in 1981 the legislature created the New Capital Site Planning Commission to develop new plans and cost estimates for capital relocation. In the 1982 general election, voters were asked to decide if they wanted to move the capital to Willow, at an estimated cost of $2.8 billion. They said no, 102,083 to 91,049. With that vote, laws and initiatives relating to capital relocation were repealed.

8

Appoint or Elect Judges?

EARLY IN DECEMBER, on the twenty-fifth day of the convention, Mildred Hermann was getting anxious. The committees were hard at work but none had yet reported out anything for the convention as a whole to consider and act on. "It seems to me," she told her fellow delegates, "those reports ought to be coming in. . . . So I am giving due warning to everybody here that if we don't get some of the work out by the first of the week I am going to become the nagging wife of this convention."[1]

On the twenty-ninth day, the proposed article on suffrage and elections came out of committee and the following day the article on the judiciary was introduced in first reading. Things were beginning to move.

The judiciary article came before the convention in second reading— open to amendment—on the thirty-second day, and Robert McNealy immediately moved to strike the section providing for appointment of judges.

"Being an Alaskan, I have lived under the appointment system for so long that I feel that I should have the right to vote for these judges," he said. Appointments "are more political than the vote of the people."

Whenever an elected judge makes a decision, "he has to keep peering over his shoulder to find out whether it is popular or unpopular," countered George McLaughlin, chairman of the Committee on Judiciary Branch (five of whose seven members were attorneys). Furthermore, he said, all modern constitutions provided for an appointed judiciary.

Under the committee plan, the state judiciary would be a unified system consisting of a three-justice supreme court, a superior court system of five judges, and lesser courts established by law—by the legislature.[2] The chief justice of the supreme court would be the administrative head of all courts. The system would closely resemble New Jersey's highly rated court system, recently modernized under that state's newly rewritten constitution.

Judges were to be appointed by the governor from among persons nominated by a judicial council of seven members: three attorneys appointed by the Alaska bar, an official territorial organization which licensed attorneys; three lay members appointed by the governor; and the chief justice, who would be chairman. Members, except for the chief justice, were to serve six-year terms. After judges had served for a prescribed length of time, voters would decide whether they should be retained.

If judges were elected, McLaughlin continued, there wouldn't be "a nonpartisan judiciary but a judiciary that in substance would be dictated [to] and controlled by a political machine."

Edward Davis had come from Idaho where judges were elected and a judge's chances of reelection might be affected by decisions he had made or "how popular his opponent might be, completely irrespective of qualifications." The judiciary committee plan, he said, is a compromise between appointing judges for long terms and electing them. It is "the best means yet devised" to select judges "and to keep [them] free from outside pressures and to get rid of judges who are not able to properly do their job."

Have other states using this plan ever voted against retaining a judge? George Sundborg wanted to know. Yes they have, McLaughlin assured him.[3]

McNealy, who had several other amendments to offer, decided against carrying on his fight when fifty-one delegates voted against his motion to do away with appointment of judges.

The convention adopted an amendment by Sundborg to require legislative confirmation of the three lay members of the judicial council but rejected an amendment by Nenana merchant and legislator John Coghill to require similar confirmation of the attorney members, thereby placing these members beyond reach of the electorate.[4] McLaughlin and Ralph Rivers opposed the Coghill amendment, arguing that if it were adopted, attorney members would be considered on the basis of their political affiliation and acceptability rather than on their professional qualifications, and the bar was best able to determine the qualifications of its members.

John Hellenthal tried but failed to persuade the delegates to make lawyers employed by the federal government ineligible for state judgeships. The judiciary committee had proposed that judicial candidates must have practiced law for five years in Alaska. Time spent in federal employment would not count toward that requirement, under Hellenthal's proposed amendment.

"I hope that in the years to come that we will see a diminution of federal officials in Alaska, and I sincerely hope it will be accelerated," Hellenthal declared, not quite on target. But then he drew his bead: "Experience has shown that people who have never practiced law and who have merely been in government jobs do not make good judges."

The delegates saw the Hellenthal amendment as discriminatory and limiting the judicial council in carrying out its task.

A motion by Sundborg to eliminate the proposed five-year practice requirement sparked the first debate of the convention on the question of residency. The state shouldn't be prevented by unnecessary restrictions from getting the best men for government service, said Sundborg. His amendment failed.

In the end, however, the five-year practice requirement for judges was dropped: the delegates adopted an amendment by George Cooper which would leave it to the legislature to decide judicial qualifications beyond the basic ones of citizenship and membership in the Alaska bar. "The people have no choice originally in the appointment or in the nomination of judges, but through...[their] representatives, their legislators, they will have the right to insist on additional qualifications," said Cooper.

Trust the Legislatures

"I think one of the fundamental things that this body is going to have to do, whether they like it or not, is to develop faith and trust in the future legislatures of Alaska."
—Mildred Hermann

Supporting the five-year requirement, Irwin L. Metcalf, a Seward grocer and former U.S. marshal, had told the convention the late delegate to Congress and U.S. district judge Anthony Dimond "was loved by everyone" because "he was a longtime resident here in the Territory. He worked with the miners out in the hills...and understood the common man's problems. He was not only a humane judge but learned in the law and I wish you people would remember that residence means something."

Douglas Gray felt the same way: The residence requirement "gives the people a chance to know who they are...[getting] for the top offices of the state."

Mildred Hermann at first had liked the five-year practice requirement but now favored the Cooper amendment leaving it to the legislature to prescribe additional judicial qualifications. And she offered this comment: "I think one of the fundamental things that this body is going to have to do, whether they like it or not, is to develop faith and trust in the future legislatures of Alaska."

So the convention hewed to its intention to avoid lawmaking and keep the constitution a basic framework of government.

Appoint or Elect Judges? / 41

Later, when the judiciary article came before the convention for a final reading, McNealy again vented his feelings regarding the appointment of judges but only five others joined with him in voting against the article.

The basic structure of the state court system has remained unchanged over the years. Legal scholars consider the system one of the nation's best. There have been several amendments to the judiciary article of the constitution, however. The independence of the chief justice of the supreme court has been reduced by providing for his selection from among members of that court by a majority of the court rather than by the governor, and he may not serve consecutive terms in office. The administrative director of the court system now serves at the high court's rather than the chief justice's pleasure. Another constitutional amendment established the Commission on Judicial Qualifications to enforce standards of judicial conduct. A later amendment changed the name of that body to the Commission on Judicial Conduct to more accurately indicate its function; it also reduced the number of judges sitting on the commission and increased the number of public members, to give the public greater influence in its deliberations.

The legislature in 1980 created a three-judge court of appeals to hear appeals of decisions in criminal cases.

9

Voting Qualifications

DURING CONVENTION CONSIDERATION of the article on suffrage and elections, Seaborn Buckalew offered a suggestion for improving the language of the section prohibiting a person "of unsound mind" from voting. He wanted to substitute the legal "non compos mentis" for "of unsound mind."

George McLaughlin responded to the suggestion with another Latin phrase, then translated it for the benefit of the delegates: "The mountains are in labor and a mouse is born." When the laughter subsided, the delegates decided against incorporating the proposed legalism in the section.

They had disposed of weightier matters on preceding days. The Committee on Suffrage, Elections and Apportionment had proposed lowering the Alaska voting age from twenty-one to twenty and relaxing the existing literacy test for voting by eliminating the requirement that voters be able to write the English language. They would only have to be able to "read or speak" the language.

Maurice Johnson thought that was too liberal and introduced an amendment that would require voters to be able to read, speak and write the English language. "It was pointed out by somebody here that every citizen who comes over from some foreign land and is naturalized must be able to read and write," he said. "Is it so much to ask that Native-born American citizens should not be able to do the same thing?"

The amendment drew heavy fire from delegates who considered it threatening to Alaska's Native people.

The ability to read and write "is no criterion of intelligence," asserted Douglas Gray, a Juneau hotel owner. The Johnson amendment, he said, would only disenfranchise a number of Alaskans who had been denied a basic education. "I see nothing but harm to our own local-born citizens with this full limitation. . . . I believe that the mere fact that you can speak the English language is sufficient."

Frank Peratrovich, a member of the suffrage and elections committee, disclosed that he was responsible for the "read or speak" phrase in the committee proposal. Some people in his part of Alaska, a few older people, "can speak and understand the English language and also can write their name and perhaps write a sentence in English, but they cannot sit down and write letters." They are citizens, made so by a 1924 congressional act, they have voted in the past under provision of that act, and they should not be denied the right to vote in the future state, he said.

M. R. (Muktuk) Marston of Anchorage, organizer and leader of the Eskimo Scouts in World War II and long a champion of the Native people, was not about to accept the Johnson amendment. "It would be a crime," he said, to deny Natives the right to vote because they could not write. Many Natives cannot write "but they use the radio, and they have good intelligence, and they are smart and smarter than a lot of our people in our big cities on the political issues that come up."

The Johnson amendment was not accepted; the committee's "read or speak" requirement was retained.

When it came to consideration of voting age, a bare majority of the delegates turned down an amendment by Victor Fischer to lower it to eighteen, then adopted one by John McNees to set it at nineteen. R. E. Robertson was unsuccessful in trying to get the body to put it back up to twenty-one.

The Right to Vote

"Anyone that is given no part of any affair naturally has an apathy. I think if they are given the right to vote you will find the apathy disappears."
—Douglas Gray

A motion by Warren Taylor to leave the question of voting age and other qualifications to the state legislature went down before a broadside from John Hellenthal: "Every state in the Union provides for the qualifications of its voters in its constitution. . . . If you leave such an important matter to the whim of the legislature, nothing but confusion, almost anarchy, would result."

Eighteen is an age when young people normally graduate from high school, said Fischer in pressing for his amendment. "We expect them to earn their living, we expect them to fight, they can get married..."

Opposing the amendment, Barrie White said, "The fact that eighteen-year-olds can fight or are called into the armed services has no relevance at all. It is the cold fact that an eighteen-year-old boy is the best fighting machine and...that he is the most easily led." White saw "no harm" in allowing a period of time to pass after graduation from high school—"a maturing period, a period of observation and a period of continued study"—before enfranchising young people. He was "a little concerned about the political machines working into the high schools and trying to capture this eighteen-year-old vote."

Victor Rivers felt eighteen-year-olds should be given the vote "on the basis of our advanced literacy and our advanced system of education, and the progress that our youngsters have made, physically and mentally.... This is the vitamin age, the irradiated milk age, the enriched food age, and at the age of fourteen now a youngster is two and a half inches taller and thirty pounds heavier than they were thirty years ago."

"My argument is to hold it at twenty..." said Maynard Londborg. "As far as the war is concerned, I certainly feel sorry for any boy who has to go at that age [eighteen] and fight...but at the same time I do not know if that necessarily means that they should vote at that age. True, medical science has probably enabled the boys and girls to be taller and bigger at a younger age. I don't know how much that has affected the growth of the brain."

"I think they [young people] would rather see the draft age raised than the voting age lowered, and I firmly believe that twenty is the best age for voting," said John C. Boswell of Fairbanks, operations manager for the U.S. Smelting, Refining and Mining Company.

Leslie Nerland, a partner in his family's retail furniture business in Fairbanks, favored the Fischer amendment. "I feel that our eighteen-year-olds...are more progressive and more interested in civic affairs and the affairs of the Territory and nation than they ever have been before, and if we give them the right to vote...they will prepare themselves ahead of time."

Responding to a comment that young people were apathetic about public affairs, Douglas Gray declared that "anyone that is given no part of any affair naturally has an apathy. I think if they are given the right to vote you will find that apathy disappears."

The extended debate was not without humorous moments. Frank Barr, opposed to giving the vote to eighteen-year-olds, told delegates: "At the age of sixteen I joined the regular Army, voluntarily. That proves I did not have good judgment at that time, and at the age of nineteen I reenlisted. That proves I did not have good judgment then.... A man begins to form better considered opinions...at around twenty."

Supporting Robertson's unsuccessful attempt to put the voting age at twenty-one, Mrs. Ada B. Wien, daughter of Nome gold miners and wife of pioneer airline operator Noel Wien, pointed out that twenty-one was the voting age in a majority of the states and she feared that congressmen and senators from those states "might frown upon our lowering of the voting age" when considering Alaska statehood legislation.

A 1970 constitutional amendment deleted altogether the requirement that voters be able to read or speak English. That same year voters approved an amendment lowering the voting age from nineteen to eighteen. The following year the federal constitution was amended to permit eighteen-year-olds to vote. In 1972 Alaska voters approved a constitutional amendment deleting the requirement that persons must reside in the state for a year to be eligible to vote.

10
Home for Christmas

EARLY IN DECEMBER, secretary Tom Stewart, ill from overwork, requested leave to seek medical treatment in Seattle. He told delegates he had been advised "to rest for a month to prevent a serious strain to my heart."[1] By resolution, they granted his request and expressed their "best wishes for a speedy recovery and a speedy return to the convention."

In ensuing days the pace of the convention quickened and the working day grew longer. Near mid-December, with half the convention time gone, the delegates were "running, not walking, between plenary sessions and the committee rooms."[2]

The legislative act authorizing the convention provided for a recess of up to fifteen days for the purpose of holding public hearings around the Territory on proposed constitutional provisions, and the delegates voted to take this recess over the Christmas holidays, beginning December 20. As this date drew near, the committees at the urging of President Egan were making a maximum effort to complete their proposals so the public would have something to consider. Drafts of most of the principal constitutional articles were in hand when the delegates left for their homes around the Territory.

It was a good time for a break. The delegates were tired and growing short-tempered. There was some wrangling and parliamentary confusion. When a motion was made to return part of one proposal to committee for further consideration, the members of that committee got their backs up, declared they'd done their work. The motion failed.

On their return to the university on January 4, the delegates greeted one another like old friends. They reported a good turnout at many of the hearings and much public interest in and support for their work. Bad weather and unusually low temperatures had limited attendance at some hearings. There were discussions of the constitution on television —a still-new communications medium—in Anchorage and Fairbanks.

Egan welcomed Tom Stewart back to the convention: "We are happy to have him back with us. We are also happy to have his wife with us. As you know, the secretary became a married man during the course of his recuperation." Amid the laughter and applause, Mildred Hermann quipped: "Is that the kind of heart trouble he had?" Stewart and Mrs. Jane McMullin had been married December 30 by the Reverend Fred McGinnis in the university president's campus home.

As the delegates got down to work again, committee chairmen endeavored to finish their morning sessions before noon so the reporter covering the convention for the Territory's newspapers would be able to file her copy on the wire before their deadlines. With evening sessions in prospect, the chairmen also advised delegates to arrange any social engagements on a tentative basis, so they could pass them up if their presence were required in Constitution Hall.

Deep cold gripped the campus in January—the temperature plummeted to a low of minus fifty-three degrees—and Warren Taylor suggested weatherstripping the windows of the daylight-basement room in which the plenary sessions were held. "If this cold weather keeps up," he said, "it is going to be disagreeable working here unless we come with our mukluks and our parkas or what have you."

In his 1956 State of the Union message, delivered early in January, President Eisenhower once again called on Congress to admit Hawaii to the Union—and once again declined to do the same for Alaska. "I trust that *progress toward statehood* for Alaska can be made in this session" was as far as he would go.[3]

The president's reference to Alaska was "ambiguous" and a "clear-cut statement" is required, said Senator Henry M. Jackson of Washington, chairman of the Subcommittee on Territories and Insular Affairs. "If the president comes out flat-footed for Alaska, we'll report both it [Alaska statehood legislation] and Hawaii out. . . . The only way the statehood issue can be resolved effectively and taken out of politics is for the president to make the same statement for Alaska and Hawaii."[4]

Representative Clair Engle of California, chairman of the House Committee on Interior and Insular Affairs, said he was "willing to give the statehood bills another try if I get definite word what the White House wants in an Alaska statehood bill and assurance that the president will sign it."[5]

The constitutional convention delegates on January 9 sent a telegram to Eisenhower signed by William Egan informing him they were drafting a constitution for the State of Alaska and hoped to forward ratified copies to him and Congress in early May "so that it will be possible as you said in your State of the Union message that progress toward statehood for Alaska can be made in this session. When the constitution has been submitted to you and the Congress we shall respectfully ask that Alaska be admitted to the Union. . . . We shall hope for your support..."

(On February 4, the next to the last day of the convention, the delegates received a reply from the president thanking them for their wire. He told them that if the Alaska constitution were ratified he was "certain that Congress will take due cognizance of it in connection with its consideration of any statehood legislation for the Territory" and he gave his assurance "that the ratified constitution will receive careful consideration by the Executive Branch.")

On the same date they sent their telegram to the president, the delegates began working regularly at night, following a full day's work. With most committee work completed, the plenary sessions, at which they took final action on proposed articles, became lengthy. The number of days remaining was chalked daily on a blackboard positioned centrally in Constitution Hall. There was less than a month to go.

11

Power to the People

THE CONVENTION'S DECISION to adopt initiative and referendum procedures authorizing the people to propose and enact laws themselves and approve or reject acts of the legislature—by petition—came after lengthy and somewhat heated debate. The body had resolved itself into a committee of the whole to discuss this matter.

Were the initiative and referendum needed? This was the basic question on which the debate turned.

At the outset, following a reading of the committee proposal by chairman E. B. Collins, there was a move to break off the discussion and poll delegates for their opinions on whether the initiative and referendum should be included in the constitution. The move was seen by some as an attempt to dump these procedures.

Muktuk Marston voiced strong disapproval of the attempt to limit discussion and urged adoption of the initiative and referendum. A vote against these procedures would indicate a lack of trust in the people, he declared. They would be "a great healthy thing to have in the hands of the people" and "if you turn down this kind of legislation you are going to be in for a lot of embarrassment and a lot of criticism."

There were valid opinions on both sides of this thorny issue.

Some felt the initiative and referendum conflicted with the republican form of government under which people elect representatives to act for them. The people had to trust the legislature, let it make the laws. The initiative and referendum were outdated, cumbersome and costly. They could be misused by special interest groups to the detriment of orderly government. The proposed restrictions on their use in the committee proposal would render them useless.

Others argued that allowing the people this tool would only enhance democracy. With a strong executive proposed for the future state, the initiative and referendum would be an additional check on executive actions. The initiative had been effectively used in some states to pass laws legislators had declined to pass. Proposed restrictions on use of the initiative and referendum would prevent their being used excessively or misused. With these procedures available, the legislature would be more sensitive to the desires of the people.

The restrictions mentioned prohibited use of the initiative to dedicate revenues, make or repeal appropriations, interfere with the judiciary or enact local or special legislation. Generally similar restrictions applied to use of the referendum.

Polls taken at the close of the committee-of-the-whole debate showed thirty-four delegates for the initiative, sixteen against; forty-two for the referendum, eight against.

When the article came before the convention in second reading, a host of amendments were put forward, some specifying the number of signatures needed on a petition to get an initiative or referendum proposition on the ballot. Most delegates didn't want to make it too difficult or too easy to achieve this.

Ultimately, delegates decided that petitions would have to bear signatures equal in number to ten percent of votes cast in the preceding general election to be accepted. These signatures would have to be obtained in at least two-thirds of the election districts so that no one district could force an issue. But perhaps it could anyway. George Sundborg pointed out that petitioners could obtain most of the signatures in one district, say Anchorage, and then just one from each of the other election districts to satisfy the requirement.

The proposed article when finally adopted also provided for recall of all elected officials, state and local. Only judicial officers were excluded from recall, and George McLaughlin had to appeal for this exclusion, declaring that to subject judicial officers to recall would completely undermine the judiciary plan adopted by the convention under which the public would vote on retention of judges.

After another lengthy debate, the delegates decided the power to amend the constitution should rest solely with the people. E. B. Collins's Committee on Direct Legislation, Amendment and Revision had proposed three methods for amending the constitution: by constitutional convention, which the legislature or the people could call; by referral to the people of proposals approved by two-thirds of the membership of each house of the legislature; and by action of two separate legislatures.

The question, said Edward Davis, is "whether the group does or does not agree that the constitution can be amended by the legislature."

James Hurley moved that the proposal providing for amendment by two legislatures, without referral to the people, be stricken. "I would prefer," he said, "to have any proposed amendment to the constitution submitted to the people."

Victor Rivers agreed with Hurley: "I don't think that we should delegate the supreme power to the legislature to alter the document by which they themselves are constituted and they themselves are governed."

Steve McCutcheon thought otherwise: "I can't see why two legislatures, if they are in accord by two-thirds, why that shouldn't be sufficient protection for the public."

The Hurley amendment carried.

The delegates adopted the committee's first two proposals for amending the constitution. The people would be given an opportunity every ten years to vote on the question: "Shall there be a constitutional convention?" Whatever constitutional changes might be made at a convention would be subject to ratification by the people.

The Initiative, Referendum and Recall and the Amendment and Revision articles of the constitution have remained generally intact without substantive amendment over the years. The initiative has been exercised by the people a number of times, most conspicuously in connection with the effort to move the state capital from Juneau. See Chapter 7, page 37. The referendum was exercised in 1968 to repeal a voter pre-registration law and in 1976 to nullify a substantial pay raise legislators had given themselves.

The voters have never considered it necessary to call another constitutional convention. In the 1970 general election, the vote on the question, "As required by the Constitution of the State of Alaska, Article 13, Section 3, shall there be a constitutional convention?" was an affirmative 34,911 to 34,472. Persons opposed to calling a convention went to court to have the vote set aside, contending the wording of the ballot question was ambiguous and implied a convention was required to be held. The supreme court agreed and set aside the vote. In the 1972 general election, responding to the unambiguous question, "Shall there be a constitutional convention?" 55,389 voters said no, 29,192 yes. In 1982, to the same question, 108,319 said no, 63,816 yes. The next vote on the question will be in 1992.

12

Fish and Game Management

THE ONE MAJOR LOBBYING EFFORT during the convention was undertaken by a number of groups, mainly sportsmen's organizations, which wished to see control of fish and game resources vested in a commission or commissions established by the constitution rather than in the state legislature. As they envisioned it, the independent commission(s) would set policy for fish and game management and hire executives to carry it out. In this manner, they maintained, these resources would be managed on a nonpolitical basis, which would insure their perpetuation.

Opponents argued that fish and game management should be in the hands of state government and the legislature, not left to a body unanswerable to the people, a body that could be just as political as one created by the legislature.

At the insistence of sportsmen, the convention invited Dr. Ira N. Gabrielson, president of the Wildlife Management Institute and recently director of the U.S. Fish and Wildlife Service, to speak to the body. He urged the delegates to place fish and game management in the hands of a bipartisan commission established by the constitution. They could "do something that has not to my knowledge ever been done before in America—you can set up a program before you have practically destroyed the resource," he said. Few delegates were impressed. Under Fish and Wildlife Service management, the Alaska salmon resource was rapidly declining.

Telegrams and letters urging and demanding establishment of the commission(s) poured in from the Alaska Sportsmen's Council, Anchorage Sportsmen's Association, Tanana Valley Sportsmen's Association, the Anchorage chapter of the Izaak Walton League and other organizations and individuals. The Southeastern Seine Boat Owners Association expressed its opposition to such commissions, called on the convention to leave fish and game management to the legislature.

The convention had "not had more communications from the

commercial fishermen...[because] it had been discussed and agreed that this matter should be left to the legislature," W. O. (Bo) Smith, a commercial fisherman from Ketchikan and chairman of the Committee on Resources, told the delegates. But as a result of the extensive lobbying by those favoring fish and wildlife management by constitutional commission, Smith said, his committee had amended its natural resources proposal to provide for it. The added section, Section 5, read: "Regulation and administration of the commercial fisheries and of the wildlife, including game fish, shall be delegated to a commission, or to separate commissions, under such terms as the legislature shall prescribe." The last phrase meant only that the legislature would determine procedures for setting up the commission(s). It would have no voice in fish and game management.

All this resulted in sharp, protracted debate at the convention which drew in William Egan, a rare thing, and indirectly involved Delegate Bob Bartlett. The battle began when the natural resources proposal came before the body and Warren Taylor moved to strike Section 5.

George Sundborg presented the main arguments for retention of Section 5, declaring that "maybe as many as 10,000" Alaskans wanted it in the constitution "and a good many of them have taken the trouble to send us letters and wires. . . . If we strike it [Section 5], we are inviting criticism and trouble, and trouble on the ratification of the constitution...and I feel with good reason, that with our heritage of fish and wildlife up here, we should be very careful. We should be more careful than any state that has ever entered the Union...to see that they are administered and regulated by commissions which would not be subject to the political control of the state as it may go from administration to administration."

Don't Fragment Government

"It seems to me that this section is very bad as it is written. It removes the whole regulation and administration of the commercial fisheries from the executive branch...and I don't believe that we want any department set up separate and apart from the other main branches of government."
—Katherine Nordale

Rising in support of Taylor's motion to eliminate Section 5, Mildred Hermann said she "would certainly hate to see a permanent part of the constitution advocating the control and regulation of any of our natural resources or any of our departments of government by the commission or board form of government."

John Coghill, also in favor of striking Section 5, pointed out the proposed executive article of the constitution would empower the legislature to place commissions at the head of government departments if it so desired and he was opposed to placing fish and game beyond the legislature's reach. "I think the legislature should have a full and free hand to do as they want because they will do what the people wish them to do."

A strong executive would take care of the matter properly because he would be sensitive to the needs and desires of the people, said Steve McCutcheon. But even if he were remiss, the legislature would respond and the people would have the initiative power. "The last reason I oppose this section," he said, "is that I dislike seeing a board enshrined in our constitution."

"It seems to me," said Mrs. Katherine Nordale of Juneau, former U.S. collector of customs for Alaska and now Democratic national committeewoman, "that this section is very bad as it is written. It removes the whole regulation and administration of the commercial fisheries from the executive branch...and I don't believe that we want any department set up separate and apart from the other main branches of government."

"I think the fish and wildlife is an important enough resource of ours [that] it should be mentioned in the constitution," said Cordova merchant John Rosswog, one of the few delegates to speak out in favor of Section 5.

Closing the debate, Warren Taylor advised the delegates that Clarence Anderson, highly respected director of the Alaska Department of Fisheries (a territorial research agency), "doesn't want it [Section 5] in the constitution" and Taylor quoted from a letter from Anderson: "The creation of boards and/or commissions for supervision of the various natural resources should be a legislative prerogative."

The delegates voted thirty-four to twenty-one to strike the section, but that wasn't the end of the matter. Several days later, Sundborg moved to rescind this action and the debate resumed.

The sportsmen "have been given the wrong impression if they have been made to believe that our wildlife will be mismanaged under the state..." said Victor Fischer. "The only way to make this matter subject to good management and regulation is to have the legislature behind it, to make sure good laws are enacted."

Mildred Hermann expressed resentment at the "flagrant" lobbying by the sportsmen's groups and added she was opposed to anything that would "abridge and curtail and disparage the rights of the legislature to make the laws for the State of Alaska."

Fish and game should be administered "by nothing less than a full department of government and not a commission of the third grade hanging off on the fringe," asserted Victor Rivers.

A basic principle of the proposed natural resources article, said William Egan, is that fish, wildlife and other renewable resources of the state were to be utilized, developed and maintained on a sustained yield basis, that is, utilized in a limited way so they would be available forever. Egan suggested this principle could not be adhered to "without the establishment of proper agencies" in the executive branch, under the governor. And there were other sections of the article he felt would safeguard Alaska's natural resources. The sportsmen, he said, had not "properly digested" what was contained in the article.

B. D. Stewart disclosed he had informed Bob Bartlett of the fish and game controversy and "got a telephone message back in which he expressed thorough disapproval of putting into the constitution this clause which we are now discussing, and he authorized me to quote him to that effect."

Summing up his case, Sundborg said: "Unless we have some clear lines drawn in the constitution which tell the legislature what kind of a system we want set up for the regulation of our fish and game, we are just throwing it out blindly, trusting to the future when we know not what that future may be. . . . We have written into the constitution already in three or four other places...provisions that there shall be commissions and boards of one kind or another. None of them...were quite as important...as the commission that would regulate the fish and wildlife. . . . I am not ashamed to bow to pressure when it is pressure from the people."

Given a chance to change their minds on one of the most controversial issues of the convention, the delegates declined to do so, voting thirty-five to twenty to stand by their earlier decision.

For many years after Alaska became a state, a board of fish and game, established by the legislature, drafted the regulations for management of these resources. Currently this function is assigned to two bodies—the Board of Fisheries and Board of Game. Management itself is the responsibility of the Department of Fish and Game, headed by a commissioner who serves as secretary of the regulatory boards. The commissioner is a gubernatorial appointee.

The natural resources article of the constitution has been amended only once, but the amendment was a substantial one. The original Section 15 stated that "no exclusive right or special privilege of fishery shall be created or authorized" in the state. This prohibition was a consequence of Alaskans' bitter experience with the fish traps, held mainly by large, nonresident corporations. The section was amended in

1972 to empower the state to limit entry into the fisheries and to promote development of aquaculture.

For years the state tried unsuccessfully to reduce the number of out-of-state fishermen in Alaska's crowded commercial fisheries. The 1972 amendment empowered it to establish limited entry programs—grant exclusive fishing rights in certain fisheries to those who had fished in them for prescribed periods of time, generally longtime Alaska fishermen. Limited entry permits are transferable and have become quite valuable, constituting a "retirement program" for fishermen. Ironically, a substantial number of these permits are now held by out-of-state fishermen. In 1987, Commercial Fisheries Entry Commission statistics show, 9,949 permanent permits were held by Alaskans, 2,550 by nonresident fishermen. The average price paid for a permit that year was $50,794.

13
Land to Natives?

MUKTUK MARSTON WANTED TO GIVE ALASKA NATIVES title to the lands they used and occupied. At a time well before there was an organized land claims movement, he appealed to the convention to provide the means of conveying these lands to them.

"This is the reason I came to this convention," he said. "I waited for two months to get here and I hope you will keep your minds and hearts open for a few minutes."

Marston said he had been trying for some time without success to help an Eskimo, George Lockwood of Unalakleet, obtain title to land on which he had long lived and fished—land being encroached upon by contractors building a radar station. The federal Native Allotment Act was ineffective. Justice demanded that the convention do something to help the Native people, he declared.

He had turned to the full body after the Committee on Resources had determined his proposal for granting land titles to Natives was beyond the scope of the convention. The committee had been sympathetic but concluded the only course open was adoption of a resolution asking the federal government to deal with the situation.

Marston's first proposed amendment to the resources article called on the state legislature to grant "equivalent homestead or other property rights" to Natives for the lands they traditionally used for fishing, hunting and trapping. His amendment, he said, was not an act to settle the larger aboriginal land claims.

John McNees was with Marston: "We must make provision for these people who have made such a great contribution to our civilization."

So was Maynard Londborg: "I think it would bear some very serious consideration."

And John Hellenthal: "Now people undoubtedly will jump up here and say how much this is going to cost us. . . . Well, you have got to take some risks with statehood and this is the kind of risk that I want to see taken."

If the amendment is adopted as written, there "won't be any [state] public domain...because certainly some Indian, some Eskimo, some Aleut had an interest either in trapping, hunting or fishing rights in every foot of Alaska at one time or another," warned Edward Davis. "In my opinion this proposed section will not do what it is designed to do. It would certainly upset the entire possibility of Alaska having any public domain and would be setting up one group of our citizens... against the rest."

The Marston amendment would create "a completely new set of property rights" which would cast a cloud over "every title in the Territory," said George McLaughlin.

After a recess, Marston came back with a substitute amendment that would have the state legislature convey "lots and small tracts" to "Indians, Aleuts or Eskimos" who had occupied or used them. "I believe that this organization...will do something about George Lockwood and people like him...All this amendment does is grant [to him] a little piece of land where he lives and the cabin site where he fishes," said Marston.

George Sundborg moved to strike the words "Indians, Aleuts or Eskimos" and replace them with "Alaskans," explaining this action by alluding to a letter to Marston in which Lockwood stated that Natives "would like to see our children grow up as any average American citizen and live with equal rights as white men." If the Marston amendment were adopted without this change, Sundborg said, the convention would be "setting...[Natives] aside as a class forever. . . . I contend that that is wrong and that we should not have it in our constitution. . . . We should have a constitution here which applies to all men equally."

"By amending it to 'Alaskans'...you've killed it," declared McLaughlin. "Because, in substance, what you're providing is that you merely split up the public domain, and by direct gift, pass it out to those present here at the time we obtain statehood."

But the convention voted to incorporate "Alaskans" in the Marston amendment.

Sundborg next proposed adding the words "native-born" before "Alaskans" to indicate obliquely that the Marston amendment was intended to aid Natives. The delegates found that proposal unacceptable. "Native-born" could refer to a non-Native born in Alaska.

When the amendment with "Alaskans" in place of Natives came up for final consideration, the convention turned it down by a vote of thirty-four to sixteen. It was too broad, too vague, the majority felt. It didn't directly address the problem Marston had brought before the convention; it could result in a giveaway of all land the future state would receive.

Recognizing the validity of Native land claims, the delegates did place in the constitution—in the General Provisions article—this language: "The state and its people...disclaim all right or title in or to any property including fishing rights...held by or for any Indian, Eskimo, or Aleut, or community thereof...[T]he property...shall remain subject to the absolute disposition of the United States."

At convention's end the delegates also adopted a resolution calling on the first state legislature "to make provision in the initial selection of lands to correct such inequities and to remove these uncertainties regarding Native homes, hunting camps, and fishing sites, by granting to qualified claimants title to them..." The resolution, which was not to "prejudice or affect presently pending aboriginal claims matters," also called upon federal agencies "to hasten the issuance of patents in all proper cases to Native land claimants, and otherwise to adjudicate Native land claims."

The state conveyed no small tracts of land to Natives under terms of the resolution adopted by the convention. By the late 1960s, Native land claims blanketed the entire state. The long-standing problem of aboriginal land claims was finally resolved in 1971 when the U.S. Congress passed the Alaska Native Claims Settlement Act. Under the act, Natives received forty million acres of land and $962.5 million as compensation for lands given up. Five hundred million dollars of the total came from federal and state mineral leasing revenues.

14

Local Government

FRANK BARR DIDN'T LIKE "BOROUGH" as the name for the regional form of local government to be established upon attainment of statehood. "I don't like the sound of it, and I think it's confusing to some people." Why not "county...but still have our own form of county government?" he suggested.

The Committee on Local Government had "not come out with any name that we were completely satisfied with" but thought that "borough" was the most reasonable because of its definition as "a town or place organized for local government purposes," replied chairman John Rosswog. The committee didn't think "county" fit the concept of the type of local government required for Alaska, he said.

The convention eventually concurred on "borough" after considering a variety of names: "county," "canton," "province," "division," "district." "Borough" sounded like "burro" or "burrow" to some delegates, "county" aroused thoughts of corruption, overlapping jurisdictions, inefficiency, "canton" made one delegate think of "tinkling cymbals or the Chinese dancing girl, the pagodas, and chop suey." "I'll ride with borough," said another delegate when the matter was put to a vote.

This light moment was one of a very few during the convention's deliberation of the local government proposal. Devising a local government system proved to be one of its most difficult tasks. Alaskans had had no experience with intermediate government, having been prohibited by the federal Organic Act from establishing counties. There was nothing between the territorial government and the cities and school and public utility districts. Some form of intermediate government would be needed in the future state. It ought to be simple, flexible and adaptable throughout Alaska and to provide for maximum local self-government.

What the delegates came up with was a system in which local government powers would be vested only in cities and boroughs.

Existing special service districts would be integrated with the borough. Cities would be part of the borough in which they were located and, like the borough, have powers conferred by law or home rule charter. Boroughs were to be organized only as the need for local services arose and the means to support them became available. The unorganized areas would be governed by the legislature, the boroughs by elected local assemblies. The state would create an agency to assist local government and a commission to adjust local boundaries.

This was the general plan, and the formidable task of implementing it was left to the future state legislature. Realizing that many problems would arise during the period of borough formation, partly because of the lack of detail in the constitutional article, the convention added a sentence providing that "a liberal construction shall be given to the powers of local government units."

Such an addition was needed, said James Hurley, because the local government article was "extremely vague, pardon the expression, as to how these things are going to be carried out, and I think it is essential that the legislature and the courts that may be confronted with the problem do construe it liberally so as to effectuate a good strong home rule...type of local government."

The cities were to be represented on assemblies by one or more of their council members and could enter into joint administrative agreements with boroughs. The convention generally believed these provisions would promote cooperation between cities and boroughs.

"We felt that in order to get integration between your city and your borough...it would be necessary to have [assembly] members from the city that were authorized to represent the city," Rosswog said.

Explaining why school board members would not sit on the assembly, Victor Fischer, another member of the committee, said: "What we wanted to avoid...was the specific seating of people with just one interest. . . . We prefer to keep this a general governing body so that everybody was interested in the general welfare of the whole borough."

The city-borough representation plan was defective, Edward Davis declared, because members of the borough assembly "are going to be representing interests and not the borough. We are going to have people there...for the specific purpose of representing the city. We are going to have other people there...representing the people outside the city."

Hurley asked Fischer if a borough would be created "without the voice of the people within the area," and Fischer responded: "The answer would be no. . . . When a certain area reaches a position where it can support certain services and act on its own behalf, it should take on the burden of its own government. . . . We don't actually visualize that the state will force...[borough organization] since we feel that they should be set up on such a basis that there will be enough inducement for each to organize." Fischer stressed, however, that it would be left to the legislature to determine how boroughs would come into being.

Maynard Londborg, another member of the local government committee, warned that borough organization should be "induced." If the legislature were to "force it upon the people I think you are going to have it taken with resentment and probably a lack of good local government."

There was considerable discussion of borough size by the convention but no finite determination reached. Population, geography, economy and transportation were factors to be considered in setting up boroughs, and each borough was to "embrace an area and population with common interests to the maximum degree possible."

The proposed borough "did not hold to any particular size," said Rosswog. Other committee members offered their views on this, Fairbanks transfer company owner James Doogan saying the borough would be large—"as large as [it] could possibly be made and embrace all of those things [common interests to the maximum extent possible]."

The borough would encompass an area "that had common interests but would not be so big as to be unwieldy...not be so small as to be expensive," said Victor Rivers. "It is a matter of the exercise of judgment which has been left to the local level with the advice and assistance of the state." Looking at the Anchorage area, Rivers envisioned a borough embracing the area "from Portage to Knik Bridge [the approximate size of the Municipality of Anchorage today]."[1]

The only major debate during consideration of the local government article had to do with the status of school districts. Elected school boards would continue to set school policy and hire administrators but some delegates thought school districts should having taxing powers as well, along with the cities and boroughs. Maurice Johnson proposed such an amendment to keep the school district "intact and operating as an independent unit."

Warren Taylor opposed the amendment, saying "the purpose of this [local government] article is to simplify our governmental procedure and also to prevent an overlapping of government functions. Now we have two government functions set up here, the cities and the boroughs. I think that is plenty. They can provide for everything including the schools."

Favoring the amendment, Edward Davis said "we will regret the day...if we do not give the schools some sort of taxing power, independent of the other agencies that are working on the other phases of government. . . . I have seen so many times where needed things that the city wants...compete with needed things that the school district wants. . . . If it comes down to a point of educating our children as against having more paved streets, I am going to take the schools."

Jack Hinckel, Kodiak petroleum products distributor, disagreed: "I think that for a school district to do anything other than to make up their budget and to submit it to the city or the borough...will throw the economy of the city and borough completely out of tune. . . . I think you will destroy the cities by permitting this to happen."

There was some discussion of the possible unification of cities and boroughs as a means of further simplifying local government. The local government committee perceived "the possibility that as the borough becomes a more definite unit of government over the years...that all functions that can best be carried out on the unified basis [could] be transferred over to the borough," Fischer told delegates.

Frank Barr made one last effort to get rid of "borough" when the local government article came up for final consideration. Pleading for some other name, he said, "I want to be able to walk down the streets without having people throw rocks at me." But "borough" survived.

A day later, he told his fellow delegates: "Yesterday I tried to put through a certain measure, which was a marked failure, and Mrs. Barr was very much concerned about my lack of success, and in order to secure a little better support next time she whipped up a big batch of fudge, and you will see two boxes on the secretary's desk."

"As a result of this gesture, I propose that at the proper time the name of 'barr-boro' be considered," said Anchorage public relations consultant Herb Hilscher.

Said a delegate unidentified in the record, amid the laughter of his colleagues: "We might consent to change the name to 'barr-o.' "

Edward Davis's contention that the city-borough representation plan was not workable proved to be correct. In Anchorage, assembly deliberations for years were marked by controversy between city and out-of-city members. The voters in 1972 approved a constitutional amendment which deleted provisions for city and noncity representation on the borough assembly, thus clearing the way for borough-wide elections.

There was great reluctance in the new state to form boroughs, and the legislature in 1963 passed the Mandatory Borough Act which required borough organization in eight areas, including Anchorage and Fairbanks, by January 1, 1964.

There are three home rule municipalities in which city and borough governments have unified: the City and Borough of Juneau, the City and Borough of Sitka, and the Municipality of Anchorage.

15
The Legislature

THE TWO HOUSES OF THE LEGISLATURE *sit together in joint session* to deal with gubernatorial vetoes? This was a unicameral procedure and not the way the territorial legislature did it. The question was debated at length—and with some heat—as was the question of what legislators should be paid.

The Committee on Legislative Branch had proposed that vetoes be considered by joint sessions. In the territorial legislature, as in the U.S. Congress, the two houses voted separately on vetoed bills. The concurrence of both was required to override a veto by the chief executive.

Chairman Steve McCutcheon explained the committee's reasoning this way: "We felt that the authority of the Senate should be diluted. . . . With a small Senate, it required so few to sustain the governor [block an override] that it gave an extremely strong executive arm more power and authority than he should have."

Maurice Johnson didn't like the committee proposal and asked the convention to reject it and retain the territorial procedure. The committee was proposing that the legislature transform itself into a unicameral body to weigh vetoes and he preferred a bicameral system, he said.

The committee proposal "almost takes the overriding out of the hands of the Senate," Maynard Londborg commented. "...They have to sit with the House that is twice as big."

Johnson's amendment failed on a tie vote but Frank Barr promptly moved to rescind this action and the debate resumed.

"All of us in Alaska...remember when...we had only eight members in the Senate...when three members of the Senate could force the will of the entire legislature, or three members...with the governor, if they happened to be his supporters, could pretty well run the show," said Burke Riley in opposing the Johnson amendment. In the proposed state legislature, he went on, seven of the twenty senators could block overriding of vetoes [on the basis of a two-thirds vote to override]. Seven out of a total of sixty legislators "would have the whip hand on any tough decision. . . . If you believe in the democratic process...that is not right."

"It is even worse than Mr. Riley says," George Sundborg followed up. With a three-fourths vote proposed to pass revenue and appropriation bills over gubernatorial vetoes, five senators could "thwart the will of the other fifty-five members."

"The question here," said Barr, "is whether we favor the unicameral or the bicameral system. . . . It would be a simple procedure to override the veto of the governor under this joint session."[1]

If the convention wants a strong executive, "then we must support the fairly strong veto, which would be the bicameral veto," said Victor Rivers.

Twenty-seven delegates voted to rescind the vote on the Johnson amendment, ten short of the two-thirds required to accomplish this. The committee proposal for joint sessions on vetoes would be adopted.

On the matter of salaries, the committee proposed an annual salary for lawmakers equal to one-third of the governor's. The future state legislature would set the governor's salary and have the option of paying itself per diem while in session.

John Boswell, fearing an annual salary would lead to excessive pay and consequently "career legislators," proposed that lawmakers be paid only for time spent in session. Under a formula he had devised, legislators could receive about $1,400 a month which, he said, "would induce a fairly high type of person to run for the legislature."

He conceded lawmakers would receive greater pay under his formula than under the committee's if sessions were to run longer than four and a half months, but he didn't believe this was likely to happen. "It may be necessary for the legislature to sit for a long time for the first year or so, but I would expect that the time will come when it might only require a month or two."[2]

Arguing for an annual salary and against the Boswell amendment, Steve McCutcheon told the delegates: "If an annual salary is established, the legislatures will conclude with as much dispatch as the public interest will permit. . . . They'll be happy to get back home. If it's put on a daily remuneration basis, then necessarily there must be a limit [to the length of legislative sessions]."

Legislators should receive an annual salary, said Victor Rivers, because "all during the time you are a member...whether you are in session or not, you spend a substantial amount of your time working with, helping people."

The Boswell amendment was defeated and the convention went on to consider—and reject—other salary proposals, based on a percentage of the governor's salary.

Alluding to the various attempts to incorporate a legislative pay formula in the constitution, Anchorage attorney Dorothy Awes (now Haaland) said "the very action we went through shows the difficulty of deciding on a percentage.... I think that it is both unwise and unnecessary to put any specific limitation in the constitution."

Frank Peratrovich agreed: "We have tried to solve this practically from all angles. It seems that we are pretty much divided, and the only solution...is to leave this to the legislative body.... They are in a better position to know...what the needs are."

Yes, said Mildred Hermann. "Right now we don't know what our revenues will be when the salary for the first legislature...will have to be set."

Finally adopted was an amendment by Seaborn Buckalew providing that lawmakers would receive annual salaries. Thus it was left to the legislature to decide how much they should be paid for their services. The delegates also decided lawmakers "may receive" per diem allowances to cover their expenses while in session.[3]

Herb Hilscher had urged rejection of the Buckalew amendment. "If we give the legislators a blank check to write their own salaries, that is the finest argument in the world to get people...to vote against ratification of the constitution."

A number of delegates warned the convention to proceed with caution on this matter, pointing out the new state would have limited revenues.

John McNees argued for substantial salaries to "bring the top men of the Territory to the foreground," especially in the formative years of the state. The salary should be sufficiently high, he said, "so that a man could become a careerist in the field. That is the only way we are going to prepare adequate men for the United States Congress."[4]

Robert McNealy had a different view: "It is an honor to sit there [in the Senate] and it should not require any salary at all. The House...is probably a little different proposition."

The convention had little difficulty deciding the state legislature should meet annually on an unlimited basis. There were some misgivings about this decision. "I think a lot of good men in the Territory that would probably run for the legislature will not under these conditions," said Wrangell drugstore owner and longtime legislator James Nolan.

George Sundborg tried to persuade the convention to set a sixty-day limit on the yearly legislative sessions. Such a session was "generous," he maintained. Territorial legislators "have been meeting only sixty days every other year."

But most delegates were convinced that unlimited, annual sessions would be a necessity once Alaska assumed the heavier responsibilities of statehood.

The Legislature / 67

Legislative sessions have often run to considerable length since statehood. The question of what to do about that situation was answered in 1984 when voters approved a constitutional amendment limiting sessions to 120 days. A 1976 amendment broadened procedures for legislative consideration of vetoed bills. The constitutional requirement that vetoes be considered by joint sessions remains solidly in place.

16

Legislative Apportionment

"I DON'T THINK THAT IF YOU WERE GIVEN THE PROBLEM of apportioning the heavens, or heaven itself, that you could please all the occupants."

Thus John Hellenthal began his explanation of his apportionment committee's plan for apportioning the House and Senate seats of the state legislature. But after the plan had been amended and finally adopted, most delegates were confident their constituents would be pleased with it—for a while.

One of the most important votes of the convention was on the amendment to the apportionment article proposed by Edward Davis, an amendment which guaranteed the rural areas representation in the Senate. Its passage forty-five to six allayed fears of urban domination of the legislature and consequently assured rural acceptance of the constitution.

The committee proposal called for the forty House seats to be apportioned among twenty-four election districts on the basis of population. Anchorage, the largest city, would get eight seats, Fairbanks, the second largest, five. The twenty-seat Senate was to be apportioned largely on the basis of area, with eight members to come from four at-large districts—Southeastern, Southcentral, Central and Northwestern—and the remaining twelve from smaller single-member districts each consisting of two House districts.

Rural delegates recognized that future reapportionment could reduce representation in the House since several of the proposed rural House districts barely qualified for representation under the convention plan, but they were not prepared to relinquish seats in the Senate. The apportionment article provided that the big at-large Senate districts would retain their total number of senators regardless of what might happen to House districts through reapportionment. The Davis amendment extended this security to all Senate districts: "The Senate districts...may be modified to reflect changes in election [House] districts. A district, although modified, shall retain its total number of senators and its approximate perimeter."

Said Jack Hinckel during debate on the amendment: "When we went home on our holiday...we explained the arrangement of the senatorial districts and assured our people that they were going to have senatorial representation no matter what happened." Mike Walsh pointed out a compromise had been reached in committee providing for Senate apportionment on the basis of area "and that compromise is exactly what Mr. Davis' amendment offers to you tonight."

Thomas Harris said he had also assured his constituents over the recess that "we may lose our House representatives...but we will never lose our senator. That was in our minds and we thought that was what the article said. We have found out that wasn't exactly what it said... and that is the reason that this amendment tonight was asked for."

"This convention has been completely free of divisions...and I venture that it is the first gathering...ever held in Alaska that was free of those divisions," said Davis. "And it seems to me that if we can assure each area...representation in the Senate, that we have accomplished what we set out to do."

That was the end of that, but Douglas Gray had made some comments that foretold the "one man, one vote" decision of the U.S. Supreme Court in 1964 requiring that both houses of state legislatures be apportioned on the basis of population. Said Gray: "The Senate lines are too strict...they should be more elastic...this is government by the people. It is not government of the mountaintops or the lakes or the flats...The plan is very acceptable at the present time...but it does not take care of populaton shifts...it is fair today...whether it is going to be fair in 1970 or 1980, I do not know."

Under the constitution, the governor, with the assistance of a reapportionment advisory board, is to reapportion the House immediately following each ten-year federal census. In compliance with the U.S. Supreme Court's 1964 decision, Governor William A. Egan reapportioned the Alaska Senate. The legislature has been reapportioned several other times in line with the constitutional requirement and with state court decisions arising from legal challenges of gubernatorial reapportionment.

17

A Strong Executive

EXECUTIVE POWER IN THE TERRITORIAL GOVERNMENT was exercised by a governor appointed by the president, several elected officials, and a number of legislatively created boards and commissions whose members were appointed by the governor and subject to confirmation by the legislature. The boards and commissions appointed executive officers to act for them on a day-to-day basis. It was difficult, often impossible, to fix final responsibility for governmental actions. But this made little difference because few in this government could be reached by voters.

The delegates to the constitutional convention wanted the future state government to be headed by a strong chief executive who would be wholly responsible for the conduct of that government. They disagreed only on how strong the executive should be. At a public hearing convened by the Committee on Executive Branch before the convention's year-end recess, Governor Heintzleman (by telegram) and Ernest Gruening urged establishment of a strong executive. "Divided authority frequently results in delays and stalemates and, in the end, the people are the ones who suffer," said Heintzleman.[1]

The convention adopted most of the proposals of the committee which, in support of the strong executive concept, recommended the election of just two officials, a governor and secretary of state. The convention decided candidates for these offices would run on their own in the primaries and the nominees of each party would run together in general elections. This way the successor to the governor would be an elected official well known to the public. The governor would be elected in an off-presidential year to minimize the influence of national politics on the election.

Wanting the strongest possible chief executive, several delegates had pressed for appointment of the second in command. Ernest Gruening had suggested the secretary of state be appointed from the cabinet.

Why a secretary of state instead of lieutenant governor?

The executive branch committee saw a lieutenant governor as "a man who has an honorary title without much work to do. . . . " said committee member Frank Barr. "Our conception of a secretary of state is a man who does work under a governor. . . . In that case he will have a knowledge of all the work that is going on and all the problems, and if he takes over as governor, he will be highly qualified."

The committee left it to the governor and legislature to organize the state government, specifying only that there were to be no more than twenty principal departments. Department heads appointed by the governor would face confirmation by the legislature meeting in joint session. The convention concurred in these proposals.

Although the committee preferred that departments be headed by appointees of the governor, it did recommend that the legislature be empowered to place appointive boards or commissions at the head of departments and other agencies. Members would be appointed by the governor and be subject to legislative confirmation. As under territorial law, these bodies would be authorized to select executive officers to act for them but these officers would have to meet with the approval of the elected governor. This recommendation was also adopted.

The convention's desire for a strong governor and dislike of boards was clearly reflected in its fifty-to-four defeat of an amendment by John Coghill which would have eliminated the requirement that an executive officer appointed by a board or commission be acceptable to the governor. His amendment, Coghill said, would keep partisan politics out of such things as education and health and welfare.[2]

If that amendment were adopted, warned George Sundborg, "we would be inviting and opening the way to principal departments of our state running wild without any reference to the policies of the governor. . . . I believe we would soon get back to government as bad and as unresponsible as we have now under the Territory."

The Coghill amendment, declared Steve McCutcheon, would strike "the very heart out of this section. We are...tired of rule by board. It may have been necessary...in past years in order to eliminate too much influence from an absentee governor, or one appointed by absentees. . . . We have created boards for the purpose of getting away from Washington, D.C. and controlling our own affairs, but when we elect our own governor...we need have no fear that politics are going to get into this."

Some delegates believed there should be more than two elected officials at the head of the state government and gave their support to an amendment proposed by Frank Barr providing for an elective attorney general.

He favored a strong executive, Barr said, but contact with

constituents had convinced him Alaskans wanted to vote for more than just two top officials. "I felt that if another official should be elected, it should be the attorney general," he told the convention. "...In case we had a governor who wanted to bulldoze something through...if it were a little bit questionable...[an appointed attorney general] might feel that he was obligated to the governor...and his opinion might be biased a little bit...so to remove him from that embarrassing position, I think that he should be elected."

If the convention accepted that amendment, it might just as well provide for election of all government officials and forget about a strong executive, countered George McLaughlin. The attorney general, he said, is just another attorney giving an opinion, and his opinions are subject to challenge in the courts. Give the governor the power to appoint his own attorney general, McLaughlin urged. "It is an attorney-client relationship and the relationship has to be based on faith and personal selection."

Ralph Rivers didn't think much of the Barr amendment either: "If we want to be sure that the strong executive...is going to get the blame if he doesn't have a successful administration, let us not give him any outs. Let's not take him off the hook by giving him an [elected] attorney general that he can put the blame on."

Barr's amendment was rejected.[3] He had planned to offer another that would make the commissioner of labor an elective official but changed his mind. "I can see this body does not believe that should be done."

The question of residency as a qualification for office-holding came up again during consideration of the executive article. The executive branch committee generally favored residency requirements and wanted department heads to be three-year residents of Alaska at the time of their appointment.

Burke Riley proposed eliminating this requirement, saying the governor should be free to recruit the best possible administrators, wherever they might be found. Committee chairman Victor Rivers disagreed. Department heads should be acquainted with Alaska's problems as well as professionally qualified for their jobs, he said.

"If we want to join the United States and be equal partners with all of our citizens, then we certainly cannot build a wall around ourselves," said Herb Hilscher.

"If he [the governor] can stand the gaff of going Outside to get somebody he thinks he needs, let him do it," urged James Doogan.

If you bring a person to Alaska "and give him high powers...it is not going to be very long before he is surrounded by his own particular group...from the area from which he came," said Rivers. "...That has been the experience of the past."

The Riley amendment was adopted thirty-eight to sixteen.

So the future state would have a strong governor. And the governor's hand was further strengthened by empowering him—in the legislative article—to strike or reduce items in appropriation bills in exercising his veto power.[4]

The executive article of the constitution has remained virtually intact since the convention. The distinction the delegates drew between a secretary of state and lieutenant governor was insignificant or imperceptible to state voters who in 1972 approved a constitutional amendment changing the title of the second-in-command to lieutenant governor. The primary duty of that official, under either title, has remained the same: to provide for and supervise state elections.

18

Moving against the Traps

"IT'S INCONCEIVABLE TO ME that any representative of the people of Alaska could think about barring any chance to eliminate fish traps. It has been a burden upon the people of Alaska for my entire life and, prior to that, on other people, and I can't see how you people can fail to include this in...[the] constitution."

Eldor R. Lee, son of a Petersburg commercial fisherman and a lifelong fisherman in that community himself, had come to the convention to press for elimination of the traps and now was exhorting his fellow delegates to abolish them. Doing so, he said, would help to win approval of the constitution. "People want the fish traps out."

From the outset of the convention it was anticipated that some proposal would be put forward to eliminate the traps, which had come to symbolize all the evils of territorial status, particularly the domination of the fishing industry by the large nonresident corporations. The traps accounted for a big proportion of the annual salmon catch—the major portion in Southeastern Alaska for many years—and most of them were operated by the absentee canning interests. Packing firms in Bellingham, Seattle, Portland and San Francisco held 383 of the 429 traps licensed in Alaska in 1948.[1] That same year Alaskans voted nearly eight to one to ban traps over a ten-year period but the vote had no legal effect.

The Fish Trap Issue

"This one issue is the thing which gave the greatest impetus to the statehood movement, which resulted in the calling of this convention. This issue is so basic and fundamental that I simply cannot conceive of any written history of Alaska without a full and complete coverage of...the impact of the fish traps on one of the greatest natural resources ever known to man."
—W. O. (Bo) Smith

Now the matter was before a convention of Alaskans drawing a blueprint for a state which would have control of the fisheries. If statehood were won, the traps were doomed. Most delegates wanted the traps eliminated but differed on how best to accomplish that. The resources article of the constitution contained a section prohibiting exclusive right or special privilege of fishery but they were not convinced this would ensure the demise of the traps.

Burke Riley urged delegates to express their will regarding the traps by resolution or ordinance rather than by constitutional provision. An ordinance, defined as temporary legislation, would be appended to the constitution but not be a part of it. "If it were to be placed in the constitution, to be there forever, I think it would detract from the dignity of the document in appearing to be a matter of permanent record of economic sanctions," he said.

Seaborn Buckalew also favored proceeding by way of an ordinance, which, he said, would make traps illegal "the day Alaska was admitted to the Union, and we wouldn't have to wait for the legislature to act."

An ordinance banning traps subsequently came before the convention, from the Committee on Ordinances and Transitional Measures, of which Buckalew was a member. If adopted it would be submitted to voters for approval along with the constitution and if approved would take effect the moment Alaska became a state. It effectively summed up the general feeling of Alaskans at the time: "As a matter of immediate public necessity, to relieve economic distress among individual fishermen and those dependent upon them for a livelihood, to conserve the rapidly dwindling supply of salmon in Alaska, to insure fair competition among those engaged in commercial fishing, and to make manifest the will of the people of Alaska, the use of fish traps for the taking of salmon for commercial purposes is hereby prohibited in all the coastal waters of the state."

John Boswell moved to strike the ordinance, saying he was certain the first state legislature would ban the traps. To do so in the constitution, he said, would give trap interests "some very strong ammunition for opposing statehood and...ratification of this constitution."

Robert McNealy was of like mind. The ordinance could hurt the cause and the first legislature undoubtedly would outlaw traps, he said. "I can't imagine any representative or senator voting against the abolition of fish traps unless he was intending to move on to Seattle right after the session was over."

Buckalew countered there was nothing to lose. "They [the absentee canning interests] have been fighting us for years anyway. . . . This just points out to them that when we get to be a state they have had it. . . . We are just trying to step in and save our heritage at the first possible moment.... Who is going to protect those fish until the first legislature is convened?"

Arguing for retention of the ordinance, W. O. (Bo) Smith reminded the convention: "This one issue is the thing which gave the greatest impetus to the statehood movement, which resulted in the calling of this convention. This issue is so basic and fundamental that I simply cannot conceive of any written history of Alaska without a full and complete coverage of...the impact of the fish traps on one of the greatest natural resources ever known to man. This impact has been so great that this resource is much closer to final destruction than most of us realize."

The Boswell motion to reject the fish trap ordinance was defeated thirty to nineteen. Defeated by a greater margin was a proposal by Victor Rivers that the convention, in lieu of adopting the trap ordinance, require the first state legislature to ban the traps. Such action would be meaningless, argued opponents. A legislature couldn't be compelled to do anything.

After the ordinance had been put in final form there was another move to delete it, this one by Barrie White, and the final debate ensued. The fish trap problem, he said, "is only one of many grievances that the people of Alaska have against the territorial form of government. It happens to be the most emotionally charged one. I think we do damage to ourselves by submitting in this case to our emotions."

Yes, it was an emotionally charged issue "and that in itself makes it worth including in the constitution," responded Victor Fischer. "Take a look at the United States Constitution. There are items in there which were included because those were grievances at the time this nation was founded." He cited the prohibition against quartering soldiers in private homes as one such item.

"You can have your name down as being against fish traps but that doesn't make for a good constitution, and I feel that it's an injustice to the total program we are pursuing here to keep this in, and so I will vote with Mr. White," said the Reverend R. Rolland Armstrong, Presbyterian minister from Juneau.

There was nothing wrong with traps, too many boats was the problem, declared R. E. Robertson, the convention's odd-man-out. "I don't agree with apparently the majority of the members of this body...I favor fish traps. I think fish traps have been one of the greatest sources of our tax money for many years." Too many boats "were ruining the industry" in Cook Inlet and Bristol Bay. Boats "coming up from Puget Sound and...California are one of the most serious menaces to our fishing industry.... It isn't the fish traps."

Truman C. Emberg of Dillingham, business agent for the Bristol Bay Fish Producers' Association, agreed there were too many boats in Bristol

Bay but pointed out many of them were operated by "the same corporations that are operating" the fish traps. "No one here has said that this trap abolition is going to be the sole answer, but we have to start somewhere on the problem of conservation of our fisheries."

Also opposed to the White amendment, Sitka merchant William W. Knight, former superintendent of the Alaska Pioneers' Home, told delegates Sitka seiners had had to give up fishing at times because traps were supplying more then enough fish for canneries.

The White amendment was defeated thirty-eight to sixteen and the ordinance banning traps finally approved by a vote of forty-six to seven.

19

Pushing for Statehood

A NUMBER OF PROMINENT PERSONS addressed the convention at various times, including U.S. Senator William F. Knowland of California, Republican minority leader ("I shall do everything I can...to expedite action on...statehood..."), Major General William F. Dean, Korean war hero ("You are right up here, the closest United States territory to our most likely enemy..."), and famed explorer Sir Hubert Wilkins ("The growing importance of the Arctic in world affairs..."). But none had made a greater impression than George H. Lehleitner, a New Orleans wholesaler of floor coverings and home appliances, introduced by William Egan as a man "who over the past few years has expended a considerable part of his time and personal fortune" to help Alaska and Hawaii gain statehood.

Lehleitner, escorted to the rostrum by Republican National Committeeman Walter J. Hickel and his Democratic counterpart Alex Miller "in a display of bipartisan support for the convention,"[1] laid before the body a unique plan for attainment of statehood. Alaska should do what Tennessee had done in 1796: after drafting a constitution, elect a congressional delegation and send it to Washington to lobby for statehood. Don't wait for Congress to pass a bill. Tennessee became a state by this means in just over two months.

The Making of a Statehood Advocate

George Lehleitner, a World War II naval officer, was distressed to find on a visit to Hawaii in 1945 that the nearly half million Americans living there were denied the full rights of citizenship when the nation was just concluding a war for human freedom, Claus-M. Naske relates in his book, *An Interpretive History of Alaskan Statehood*. On becoming a civilian, Lehleitner campaigned for Hawaiian, then Alaskan statehood. Hawaiians declined to adopt the Tennessee Plan, considering it too aggressive.

Lehleitner praised the convention for its dedicated effort and predicted a model constitution would emanate from it. But "more than the drafting of a splendid constitution" would be necessary to win statehood. Hawaii, he pointed out, "had drafted a fine constitution" but that document "has been collecting dust in the Hawaiian archives building for almost six years."

He had come to Alaska prior to the convention to present his Tennessee plan. He met with a number of delegates and won the support of the *Fairbanks Daily News-Miner. The Anchorage Daily Times* didn't consider the plan feasible. Lehleitner subsequently wrote congressmen known to favor statehood to acquaint them with the plan and received encouraging replies, copies of which he distributed to convention delegates.[2]

Just before Lehleitner's appearance at the convention, Delegate Bob Bartlett sent a telegram urging delegates to adopt the Tennessee Plan. He had carefully assessed the situation in Congress, he said, and was convinced the statehood cause would be assisted if Alaska were to send a Tennessee Plan delegation to Washington. The prospects of attaining statehood by a traditional approach were "bleak." Moreover, interest in statehood was waning. The plan "might well shorten the long road to statehood." Bartlett's endorsement ensured its favorable consideration.[3]

Lehleitner agreed the statehood drive had lost momentum and told the convention the Tennessee Plan could start it moving ahead again. Six other territories had followed Tennessee's lead and all gained statehood within two years, he said. Alaska's adoption of the plan would be "big news, and the justness of Alaska's case would...move from the editorial page to the front page." He saw little chance of failure "if you sent the right men [to Washington] and they did the proper work and received the proper enthusiastic support from Alaskans." He was given a standing ovation when he concluded and later made an honorary member of the convention and designated "honorary ambassador of good will from this convention to the people of the United States and to the members of Congress."[4]

When a draft Tennessee Plan ordinance came before the convention, a motion to strike it was made, with the objective of determining the body's feeling for it. Fifty-three delegates, all of those present, voted to retain the plan.

The thorniest problem in working it out had to do with the nomination of candidates for Tennessee Plan "senator" and "representative." Should they be nominated in the Territory's next regular primary election on April 24, 1956, or by party convention later in the year?

Few favored the latter method but it had to be considered because the existing deadline for filing declarations of candidacy for the April 24 primary was February 1, before the scheduled end of the constitutional convention, and no funds were available for a special election. The proposed ordinance provided for nominations by primary election or party convention. A new deadline of February 20 was set for filing for office, and the convention nominating procedure, permitted under territorial law, would be used if the primary plan could not be followed for legal or administrative reasons.

In an attempt to put the constitutional convention on record as favoring the party convention method of nominating candidates, under which the political parties would bear all costs, George McLaughlin moved to delete all reference to nomination by primary election.

The Committee on Ordinances and Transitional Measures had provided for the alternative of nomination by convention because there was "a very slim chance of the primary system working," said chairman Robert McNealy. Committee member Seaborn Buckalew added that the committee wanted to use the primary machinery if at all possible but became convinced it would not work. For one thing, he said, there was a legal question as to whether the convention could change the existing deadline for filing for office.

A Tennessee Plan delegation of outstanding Alaskans should be sent to Washington at the earliest time but "I doubt that the kind of men we are talking about could possibly make up their minds [to run under] this primary procedure," said B. D. Stewart of Sitka. Urging support of the McLaughlin motion, the retired mining engineer said party conventions with the eyes of Alaskans focused on them would produce good candidates.

"Even if we had the money, even if it were legal, and even if we had time, I believe it would be ill-advised to elect the people who would be our members of the Congress at the very same election where voters would be casting their ballots for or against the Tennessee Plan," said George Sundborg. "Inevitably, the plan would become involved with personalities."

"I have had a good deal of experience in the process of sending ballots out for both primary and general elections, and I am convinced that there is absolutely no possibility of getting ballots out in an orderly fashion," said Katherine Nordale, speaking against the proposed primary and for the convention process. Party conventions are broadly based with their beginnings in local precinct caucuses, and independents may run for Tennessee Plan offices. "So I don't think anyone has any need to fear not getting good representation."

Some delegates were unalterably opposed to the McLaughlin motion, feeling that they could not bring themselves to deny the people the right to nominate candidates in a primary election, that under the party convention plan only "politicians" would be elected, and that the Tennessee Plan would be rejected by the people if they had no part in the nomination of candidates. But the motion was adopted.

The matter wasn't finally resolved yet. When the Tennessee Plan ordinance came up in second reading, John Rosswog moved to delete it, saying no one knew what it would cost the Territory and he firmly believed candidates should be nominated in a primary election.

Most delegates favored a primary but it wasn't possible to nominate candidates that way at this time and the alternative, to wait two years for the next regular election, would defeat the purpose of the Tennessee Plan, countered Barrie White. "The next logical step," he said, was to go after statehood. "Else why have we spent $300,000 and come here to write our constitution at the earliest possible date?...A consideration that possibly Mr. Rosswog is overlooking is that what small sum is necessary to carry out the Tennessee Plan will be many times repaid...by gaining statehood at an earlier date."

Alaskans would get to vote on the ordinance, and "as far as the cost goes, I don't think we can afford to be without statehood," said Victor Rivers.

The Rosswog motion was defeated and when the ordinance, its name changed to the Alaska-Tennessee Plan, came up for final consideration it was adopted forty-seven to five.

So the delegates had involved themselves directly in the fight for statehood and taken an important first step toward securing it.

20
A Little Militancy

As the convention neared an end, Muktuk Marston declared in an impassioned speech that Alaska should become an independent nation if it were not soon made a state—or look into the possibility of joining Canada. The delegates applauded when he finished, recognizing his remarks for what they were: an extreme expression of the frustration many Alaskans felt over the long denial of the full rights of citizenship.

This same frustration was implicit in the proposal subsequently introduced by the Committee on Ordinances and Transitional Measures calling upon the territorial legislature to put the constitution into effect and provide for the election of officers mentioned therein if it had been ratified and Alaska had not been made a state by the fourth Monday of January 1959.

The committee had voted to introduce the proposal, said chairman Robert McNealy, because "we didn't want to put in another proposed ordinance [providing] that if we were not granted statehood within a period of two years that a plebiscite should be made to the United Nations to declare us a sovereign nation. We thought that might be just a step too far."

Defiance Gains Nothing
"If we should take action as suggested in [this proposal], it would be a defiant action, and I don't believe statehood will ever be acquired for Alaska in a defiant manner."
—Leslie Nerland

Quipped John Hellenthal: "I wonder if, as a substitute...the committee gave thought...to providing for a hunger strike?"

But the committee was serious. Member James Hurley was aware the proposal was being joked about by some, but, he asked, "what are we going to do if these people [the Alaska-Tennessee Plan delegation] are not seated, if we don't become a state? Forget the whole thing? Or are we going to have another punch ready...if it is necessary? I don't think this is revolutionary. I think it is sensible."

John Coghill didn't think so and moved to strike the proposal.

Steve McCutcheon rose to its defense: "If we do not get it [statehood] by January 1959, we must take another step, go further, set up our own statehood constitution, set up our own judiciary, anything that isn't in absolute conflict with the laws of the United States, and proceed as if we were a state; elect again new members to go to Congress; and by that time I am sure the will of the people of the whole United States will properly have expressed itself so that Alaska will become the forty-ninth state..."

George McLaughlin was appalled at this development: "This convention...has maintained a high level of maturity, and without a great deal of emotionalism.... We are now in the position of school children and, having beseeched Congress and made preparations to send our representatives before that august body, we are now sticking out our tongue at them...and telling them what we are going to do. There is no validity, there is no assurance of anything under this [proposal]. It...can make us the laughing stock of the Territory.... We should...strike it as an insult to all Alaskans."

Retorted McNealy: "In speeches throughout the United States in 1775 and 1776, if the emotionalism was immaturity in those people or if they hadn't been emotional and immature, we wouldn't...[be] citizens of the United States today." If he were a member of the legislature in 1959 and Alaska hadn't achieved statehood, "you will hear some Patrick Henry speeches...and I, for one, will...[be willing to] declare ourselves a republic."

"The main thing that this [proposal] does..." said James Doogan, "is point up to those people in Congress that we want statehood as our right.... and we are going to keep rapping on their doors until they get so tired of seeing us that they are going to admit us."

Said Hellenthal: "I am proud of Alaskans because we respect the laws and we follow the orderly intelligent route in attaining our ends.... I can't see that anything can be gained by adopting this wild course of conduct.... Had we been under the iron heel of a tyrant and...been held back for years and years and years, then revolutionary language might properly be used but it certainly is out of place at this time."

What would the elected governor and secretary of state do if the constitution were activated? Ralph Rivers asked. "Are they going to move in and move out the federally appointed governor and take over his office? What purpose can they serve or perform? We can't reconstitute the courts because the courts are created by Congress. We have to become a state before we can create the courts. . . . We certainly are not going to be able to do anything except perhaps elect a state legislature...which can't take the seats of the territorial legislature until we get to be a state. Now the question is: How foolish can we make ourselves look? And that is not based on immaturity or emotion. That's only based on the proposition that wise men can make mistakes."

Maynard Londborg also considered the proposal ludicrous. "I'd like to know how in the world we are going to back up [this proposal] when the time comes. Are we going to mobilize or start building jets or something like that?"

The convention took "bold action" in adopting the Alaska-Tennessee Plan, said Leslie Nerland. "I think the action was proper, it was orderly action, and it is an action, I think, that will bring results. If we should take action as suggested in [this proposal], it would be a defiant action, and I don't believe statehood will ever be acquired for Alaska in a defiant manner."

"I have had no expression that they [those who elected him] would...authorize...any action such as this," said Eldor Lee.

Closing the debate on his motion to strike the committee proposal, Coghill asserted that voters would reject the constitution if the proposal were made part of it. Adopting the proposal, he added, would be tantamount to saying the Alaska-Tennessee Plan would not work. "I think the pressure that we can bear on Congress...with our two senators and representative, and with a good constitution behind it and with the full faith of the Alaska people, we will be able to obtain statehood."

The Coghill motion was approved thirty-seven to sixteen. A substitute proposal requiring the territorial legislature to "enact such additional measures as in its judgment are necessary and proper to assure attainment" of statehood if the Alaska-Tennessee Plan should fail to bring it was next considered by the convention. This more moderate proposal, which many delegates felt would do nothing, was defeated twenty-six to twenty-three.

BARRIE WHITE, president of Operation Statehood, standing at right, visits with Alaska Statehood Committee. Holding up Alaska's flag are E. L. (Bob) Bartlett, left, the Territory of Alaska's delegate to Congress, and *Anchorage Daily Times* editor and publisher Robert B. Atwood, chairman of the committee. Other committee members, from left, William L. Baker, Mildred Hermann, Frank Peratrovich, Percy Ipalook (Presbyterian minister and first Eskimo to serve in territorial legislature), Warren A. Taylor, Victor C. Rivers, and Andrew Nerland (father of constitutional convention delegate Leslie Nerland). *Bob Bartlett Collection, Alaska Archives, University of Alaska, Fairbanks.*

CONVENTION OPENS. Governor B. Frank Heintzleman opens the Alaska Constitutional Convention on November 8, 1955. On the platform, clockwise from left, are Dr. Neil Hosley, dean of the University of Alaska; the Reverend George Boileau, S.J.; Brigadier General T. Allen Bennett, commanding general, Ladd Air Force Base (now Fort Wainwright); Fairbanks Mayor Douglas Preston; J. Gerald Williams, territorial attorney general; Andrew Nerland, president of the university's Board of Regents; Robert Atwood, publisher of the *Anchorage Times*; Bob Bartlett, Alaska's delegate to Congress; Ernest Gruening, former Alaska governor; Dr. Ernest Patty, president of the university; Hugh Wade, treasurer of Alaska; Dr. James Ryan, superintendent of Fairbanks schools; Kenneth Carson, UA student body president; Eva McGown, Fairbanks' official hostess; the Reverend Roy Ahmoagak; and U.S. District Judge Vernon Forbes. *Fairbanks Daily News-Miner*.

READY TO GO TO WORK. The constitutional convention's legislative branch committee discusses its work on camera in the Fairbanks studio of television station KTVF. From left, the members are George Cooper, Jack Hinckel, John McNees, committee chairman Steve McCutcheon, Helen Fischer, Dora Sweeney and Eldor Lee. *Fairbanks Daily News-Miner.*

CONVENTION LEADERS. The convention's leadership and staff posed early in the convention. President William Egan, center foreground, is flanked by vice president Frank Peratrovich, left, and Ralph Rivers. Standing, from left, are Mildred Hermann, temporary convention president pending election of permanent officers; Doris Ann Bartlett, librarian; Thomas Stewart, convention secretary; and Katherine Alexander (Hurley), chief clerk. *Fairbanks Daily News-Miner.*

AUTOGRAPH SESSION. During a break in the proceedings, students from Fairbanks schools collect autographs from convention delegates Helen Fischer, left, John Cross, Peter Reader, Thomas Harris (standing behind Reader) and Maynard Londborg. *Fairbanks Daily News-Miner.*

IN SESSION. Delegate James Doogan addresses the constitutional convention as visitors watch from a gallery behind a glass partition on the campus of the University of Alaska at Fairbanks. *Fairbanks Daily News-Miner.*

IN RECESS. Delegates share a light moment during a recess in the convention. From left are John Hellenthal, George McLaughlin, Robert McNealy (behind McLaughlin), Leslie Nerland, Steve McCutcheon, William Egan (seated), John Coghill, chief clerk Katherine Alexander (Hurley) and Dorothy Awes (Haaland). *Steve McCutcheon.*

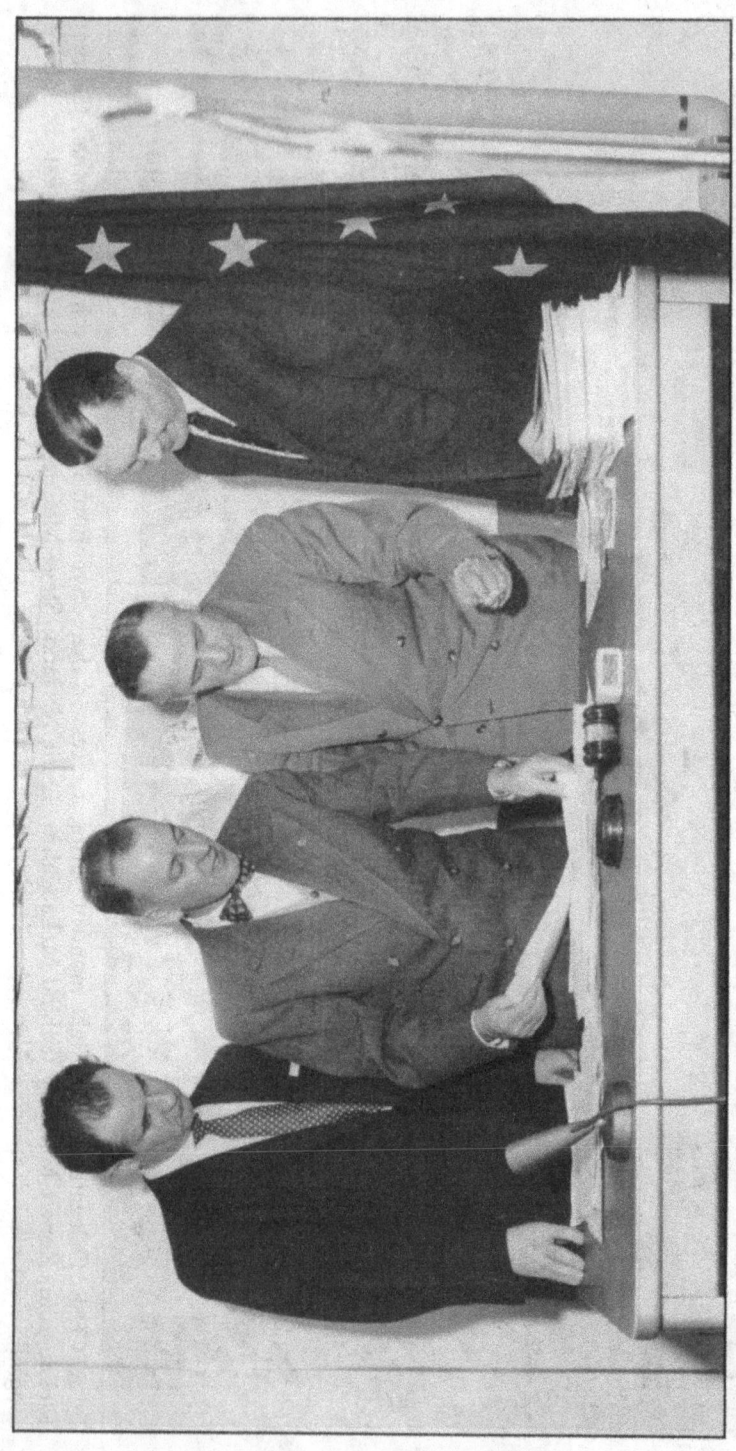

BIPARTISAN SUPPORT. New Orleans businessman George Lehleitner, second from left, assembles his notes prior to addressing the convention. He urged delegates to adopt the Tennessee Plan — to elect an unofficial congressional delegation to lobby for statehood in Washington, D.C. He is escorted by Republican National Committeeman Walter J. Hickel, right, and Hickel's counterpart, Democrat Alex Miller, in a show of bipartisan support for statehood. *Steve McCutcheon.*

DAILY COUNTDOWN. As the convention nears an end and the pace of the delegates' work picks up, the number of days remaining are chalked on the blackboard each morning. *Fairbanks Daily News-Miner.*

FULL SESSION. The convention meets in plenary session in the daylight basement of the new student union building, renamed Constitution Hall by University of Alaska Regents at the close of the convention. The committees worked in small rooms on the upper floor of the building. *Ralph J. Rivers Collection, UA Fairbanks archives.*

FORMAL PORTRAIT. Convention delegates, from left, front row: Douglas Gray, George Cooper, John Coghill, Yule Kilcher, Warren Taylor, James Hurley, Edward Davis, James Doogan, George Sundborg, Victor Fischer, Robert McNealy; seated: John Rosswog, R. Rolland Armstrong, Katherine Nordale, H.R. VanderLeest, Dora Sweeney, B.D. Stewart, Mildred Hermann, Frank Peratrovich, William Egan, Ralph Rivers, Helen Fischer, William Knight, Dorothy Awes (Haaland), Frank Barr, Ada Wien, M.J. Walsh, Eldor Lee; standing: Peter Reader, Seaborn Buckalew, Barrie White, Truman Emberg, Irwin Metcalf, John McNees, E.B. Collins, W.O. Smith, Maynard Londborg, John Boswell, Leslie Nerland, George McLaughlin, M.R. Marston, John Cross, Thomas Harris, Maurice Johnson, Jack Hinckel, James Nolan, John Hellenthal, Leonard King, Chris Poulsen, W.W. Laws, Herb Hilscher, Burke Riley, R.E. Robertson, Steve McCutcheon, Victor Rivers. *Reuel Griffin Collection, UA Fairbanks archives.*

FLAG DESIGNER HONORED. President William Egan, left, introduces Aleut Benny Benson at the convention's closing ceremony. As a young boy living in an orphanage, Benson had designed Alaska's flag. Delegate M.R. "Muktuk" Marton, right, escorted Benson to the platform.
Steve McCutcheon.

ALASKA'S NEW STAR. Anchorage Fur Rendezvous Queen Rita Martin (later Mrs. Mike Gravel) adds a 49th star to the field of a huge flag draped across the front of the federal building in downtown Anchorage. The local Elks Club had provided the flag as part of Anchorage's celebration on June 30, 1958, following congressional passage of the Alaska statehood bill. *Ward Wells Collection, Anchorage Museum of History and Art.*

STATEHOOD CELEBRATION. Anchorage residents gather on the city's Park Strip for a bonfire celebration following passage of the Alaska statehood bill by Congress on June 30, 1958. The action touched off celebrations throughout the territory. *Ward Wells Collection, Anchorage Museum of History and Art.*

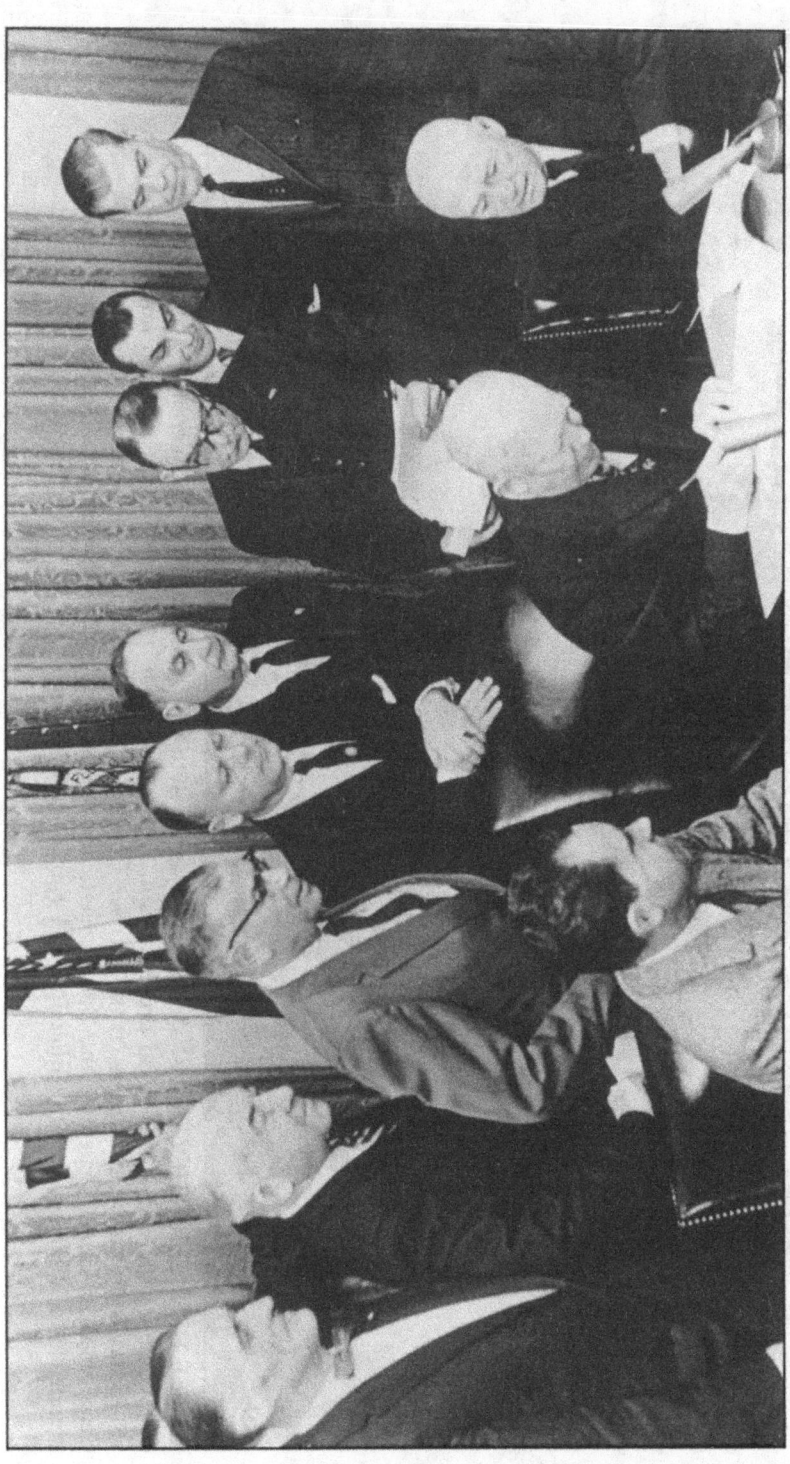

PROCLAIMS ALASKA STATEHOOD. President Dwight D. Eisenhower, with House Speaker Sam Rayburn and Vice President Richard Nixon seated beside him, signs the Alaska statehood proclaimation on January 3, 1959. Looking on from left are Congressman-elect Ralph Rivers, Senators-elect Ernest Gruening and Bob Bartlett, Interior Secretary Fred Seaton; Waino Hendrickson, who has just lost his job as acting territorial governor; David Kendall, counsel to the president; former Alaska Territorial Governor Mike Stepovich, and *Anchorage Times* publisher Robert Atwood. *Bob Bartlett Collection, UA Fairbanks archives.*

CAUSE FOR JUBILATION. Alaska's admission as the 49th state was hailed in this ceremony at the White House following signing of the statehood proclamation. *Anchorage Times* publisher Robert Atwood holds out the new flag to display a 49-star field. Others, from left, are Congressman-elect Ralph Rivers, Interior Secretary Fred Seaton, Senators-elect Ernest Gruening and Bob Bartlett, and former Territorial Governors Mike Stepovich and Waino Hendrickson. *Ralph J. Rivers Collection, UA Fairbanks archives.*

21

The Final Days

SINCE JANUARY 9 THE DELEGATES had been working day and night, mostly in plenary session, to complete the drafting of the various constitutional articles. They had learned to work methodically and deal effectively with issues as they came up. They made their way to Constitution Hall each day in darkness and deep cold. They no longer had time for social functions but school district classes and individuals continued to visit the convention, watching from behind a glass partition and listening to the discussions, which came to them through a speaker system. From time to time the delegates invited student groups to lunch with them in the cafeteria upstairs.

On January 20, former President Harry Truman sent greetings to the convention: "I sincerely hope the constitutional convention will be a successful one. I have always been in favor of statehood for Alaska and I am still in favor of it. If you have a constitution ready to present to the Congress...you will be way ahead of things."[1]

Some 3,000 invitations to convention closing ceremonies had been sent out—to President Dwight Eisenhower, members of Congress, governors of the forty-eight states, federal and territorial officials in Alaska, delegates' constituents. It was the thought of delegates that this was a means of publicizing what they were doing, of advancing the statehood cause.

The ceremonies would be held in the university gymnasium, where the convention opened. The delegates would have preferred to conclude in the basement room of Constitution Hall where all of the plenary sessions had been held since the beginning but recognized that was not possible. "This room is where our heart is but there's no room for the public here," said James Doogan. "It's the people's constitution we're going to be signing. They should have a chance to be present."[2]

With constitutional articles now coming rapidly from the convention, the work was piling up on the staff and the style and drafting committee, whose task it was to polish the articles and return them to the full body for final scrutiny.

On the night of January 25, tempers grew short as delegates perused the Declaration of Rights and noted what seemed excessive language changes. Heavy criticism was leveled at the committee and a number of amendments were proposed to undo its work—to reinstate language adopted by the convention. Near midnight, an exasperated Edward Davis, a member of the committee, moved that the committee be discharged on grounds it hadn't the confidence "of very nearly fifty percent" of the body. It was a bad moment. The convention didn't lack confidence in the committee, said Seaborn Buckalew. "We have been working hard and our nerves are a little shattered and we're getting tired."

"Rankled by too much work and too much blessed compromise, the braces holding the constitutional convention together momentarily popped loose last night during a five-hour tussle ending at midnight in an atmosphere of cleared air," wrote *Fairbanks Daily News-Miner* reporter Florence Douthit.

"More than two months of agreement for the sake of success took its toll at Wednesday's harassingly long night session when delegates started worrying over every phrase changed by the style and drafting committee for the sake of consistency and respectability of prose.

"It was a night of brittle witticism and strong minority voicings. . . . "[3]

Equilibrium was regained when William Egan ruled Davis's motion out of order, pointing out the committee was a permanent committee of the convention.

"It was a hard night all the way around but one in which an understanding was reached on the problems of the style committee and the demands of the authors of the original articles," Douthit concluded her report.

On February 3, three days before the final gavel came down, delegate R. E. Robertson went home to Juneau after sending off a letter of resignation to William Egan.[4] His "sincere convictions and beliefs" would not permit him to vote for or sign the constitution, he wrote. He didn't like the unicameral features of the constitution or the legislative apportionment article which, he said, discriminated against all areas of Alaska but the Anchorage area. Annual legislative sessions would be a "disservice" to Alaska and the initiative and referendum provisions were incompatible with the representative form of government. The fish trap ordinance was "in effect penal."

Back in Juneau a day later, Robertson announced he had resigned and stressed it wasn't a "spur of the moment" act. He had stayed at the convention, he said, to fight for designation of Juneau as the capital of the future state.[5] He did officially remain a delegate, however. His letter of resignation didn't reach Egan until 10:30 a.m. on February 6, half an hour after final adjournment of the convention.⁶ (Several years later, in poor health, he expressed a wish to sign the constitution, and several delegates visited him in his Juneau home, bringing an official copy which he solemnly signed.⁷)

The day Robertson bolted, the convention at the request of style and drafting committee chairman George Sundborg began a final proofreading of the entire constitution so the document could go to the printer that night. It had to go then, Sundborg explained, so the ink would be dry enough to permit assembly of the official copies—to be printed on a special parchment—in time for signing two days later. At that late date, some substantive changes were made in the constitution, one of which empowered each house of the legislature to expel a member on a two-thirds vote.⁸

On February 4, the seventy-fourth day, the delegates welcomed an Operation Statehood delegation which had come in on two chartered airplanes and gave the privilege of the floor to the organization's president, Ancil Payne, who pledged an all-out effort to win ratification of the constitution. "Thank God we have men and women like you doing this splendid work," he concluded.

And, finally, out of deference to the oldest member of the convention, the delegates called on E. B. Collins to initiate the adjournment process. "I move that this convention now consider adoption of the Constitution for the State of Alaska in its present form," said Collins. Mike Walsh seconded the motion. The final roll call vote on the question would come at the closing ceremonies the next day.

22

A Constitution for Alaska

THERE WERE TWO EMOTIONAL ENDINGS to the Alaska Constitutional Convention—a ceremonial one in the University of Alaska gymnasium on Sunday, February 5, 1956, witnessed by some 1,000 people, and the last meeting of the delegates the following morning in nearby Constitution Hall. The first saw the constitution for the future state finally adopted and signed, the last afforded the delegates the opportunity to reflect on what they had accomplished together and to bask in the warmth of the many fast friendships made during their long labors.

An estimated 500 persons had to be turned away from the gymnasium on Sunday. All 765 seats were occupied and more than 200 persons stood tightly together at the rear of the small gymnasium and in the galleries along each side. All of the delegates but one were present for this historic moment. They occupied the front rows of seats. Family members and friends sat behind them. Before them was a small office table bearing the constitution, a jade, silver and gold lamp which had been provided by Muktuk Marston, extra pens, ink and scratch paper. Beyond, on a low platform, was another table at which the convention officers sat—William Egan flanked by Frank Peratrovich and Ralph Rivers. At one side was the university band and at the other the Ladd Air Force Base Choral Group.[1]

A telegram had come from Bob Bartlett and it was read to the gathering. "...Today, when you sign the document which you have fashioned, there is, I believe, general understanding not only that you have worked diligently, faithfully, and with civic virtue, but also successfully, in writing a constitution dedicated to the best American principles and to the furtherance of the mighty state to be. . . . " wired the man who would be the Territory of Alaska's last delegate to Congress.

Inspired Achievement

"Fifty-five individuals of varied backgrounds, temperaments and ideas, and representing different regions and vocational groups with diversified interests, were brought together to consider the most complicated of social and political problems and blend them into a harmonious entity. By some wonderful alchemy which defies definition, this has been accomplished."

—Governor B. Frank Heintzleman

Egan introduced Benny Benson, the Aleut who as a young boy living in an orphanage designed Alaska's flag, and then designated four convention delegates to escort B. Frank Heintzleman to the rostrum. The governor, a federal appointee often accused by leaders of both political parties in Alaska of being a statehood opponent, received a standing ovation when he concluded his brief address.

The constitution about to be adopted, he had said, was the end result of "a fascinating social process. Fifty-five individuals of varied backgrounds, temperaments and ideas, and representing different regions and vocational groups with diversified interests, were brought together to consider the most complicated of social and political problems and blend them into a harmonious entity. By some wonderful alchemy which defies definition, this has been accomplished."

The constitution would "demonstrate to Americans everywhere the character of political and social thinking to be found in Alaskans," the governor went on. "We are confident that any comparison that may be made with the people of the several states will show that the plane of our thinking is as high as that of any other unit of the Nation."

Now, he said, the delegates must work for ratification of the constitution, must acquaint the voting public with its basic principles and terms. He warned that like those who drafted the national constitution, they would likely be called on to answer charges by special interest groups that the document was imperfect, but just as Alexander Hamilton responded to such charges, they could say: "I never expect to see a perfect work from imperfect man."

Heintzleman concluded: "I do not doubt that the names of you delegates and your accomplishments here will be featured in histories of Alaska for a long, long period of time."

Now the time had come for adoption of the constitution and Egan put the question to the delegates: "Shall the proposed Constitution for the State of Alaska be agreed upon by the convention?" All fifty-four delegates present voted in the affirmative, then one at a time, Egan first, amid the snap and flaring of many flashbulbs, they stepped forward to sign the document.

Egan "shook so hard as he signed the constitution that he finally dropped the pen in disgust [and] others who followed were equally as overwhelmed by the moment," the *Fairbanks Daily News-Miner* reported.[2]

"...Nothing less than a miracle from Thee has kept us together in mind and spirit. . . . " intoned the Reverend R. Rolland Armstrong, called upon by Egan following the signing to give a dedicatory prayer on behalf of the convention. "The anvil has rung with the hammer of compromise, and there has come forth a statement of our belief. Today we place the work of our hands before Thee. We ask Thy blessing as we dedicate this constitution. . . . We ask that it may speak our hearts, that it might find favor before Thee and the people of this Great Land. . . . "

Then Egan turned the gavel over to Frank Peratrovich and addressed the gathering, reciting the wrongs suffered by Alaskans as residents of a territory and declaring they had served their apprenticeship and were entitled to statehood. He concluded: "To those who say, 'No one is holding us forcibly in territorial status, we can move out if we choose,' we say, 'No, no one is forcibly holding us here. But we have built our homes here, we are rearing our children here, a great many of us will die here, we never intend to live anywhere else. We love our great United States of America, and our hearts belong too to our great Territory of Alaska, and we will never have a true peace of mind until we are taken in...as one of the great states of the Union. . . .' " A ringing, heartfelt declaration, it won prolonged applause.

There were tears in many eyes as the Ladd Choral Group sang "Alaska's Flag," concluding the ceremonies.

Afterwards the delegates reconvened in Constitution Hall to sign copies of the constitution and consider a number of resolutions and other unfinished business of the convention. In the evening they were guests of honor at a dinner in the upstairs cafeteria given by Dr. Ernest Patty and the university.

Most of the resolutions adopted by the convention in the last days expressed the delegates' gratitude for services rendered and hospitality accorded them—by their staff,[3] consultants, the university and student body, the people of Fairbanks, to mention a few. The "faithful wives of the convention" who spent many an hour in the Constitution Hall visitors' gallery were also recognized by resolution.

Two resolutions were of special importance. One authorized William Egan to complete the work of the convention, using unexpended funds (more than $30,000) and such staff as necessary to have copies of the constitution and an explanatory summary printed and distributed widely; to arrange for the printing and distribution of official ballots for the April 24 ratification election; to arrange for the orderly filing of convention records. The second resolution authorized Egan to prepare credentials for the Alaska-Tennessee Plan delegation that all hoped would go to Washington at year's end to lobby for statehood.

Another resolution adopted by the convention presented the case for "immediate statehood" and requested the president and Congress to review the state constitution and upon its ratification admit Alaska to the Union. The Alaska Statehood Committee was commended for its support of the convention and urged "to proceed immediately with studies required in planning for the transition from territorial to state government and to expand those activities which might speed...statehood."

The delegates met for the last time on the morning of February 6 in Constitution Hall. Finances were discussed, a few more resolutions were approved. They decided that forty of the original one hundred copies of the constitution would go to Alaska's public libraries and high schools and the Library of Congress. Each of the delegates received his own copy.

Recalling "the kindness that you and your faculty and student body...have extended to us," Egan presented to Dr. Patty, for the university, one of the parchment copies of the constitution and the convention gavel. "I am extremely pleased to accept these," the educator responded. "Our labors have been a labor of love, and you can realize how much we have appreciated having you here, and how much we think of the fine efforts and the fine accomplishments you have made."

Then it was Egan's turn for recognition.

Chosen to speak for the convention, James Hurley paid the delegates' respects "to our great beloved president, William Egan, for a job well done. . . . [for having] carried the whole convention forward in a way that no one else could possibly have done." The delegates had commissioned Los Angeles artist Christian von Schneidau to do a portrait of Egan and now they presented it to him together with a resolution, read by Ada Wien, praising him for "his parliamentary skill, his unwavering fairness, his personal friendliness and his untiring devotion to duty..."

Following a standing ovation, Egan, visibly moved, responded: "All I can say is that I certainly appreciate it. I will never forget a single one of you. You have done a wonderful job."

Commented the *News-Miner:* "The personality exercising a constant influence on each delegate has been that of William Egan, admired by all delegates as the best of all possible choices for president of the convention. In a spirit of fun and fairness, he controlled without bossing and never allowed reasoning to be replaced by scoffing."[4]

In the end the *News-Miner* reporter herself was honored for her "fine news coverage" of the convention. For most of the seventy-five days of the convention, her reports not only appeared in her newspaper but were filed on the Associated Press wire for use by news media around the Territory.

Given the privilege of the floor, Florence Douthit, seven months pregnant, was accorded a standing ovation when she moved forward to shake hands with Egan. In presenting a gift to her on behalf of the convention, George Sundborg said: "Mrs. Douthit...we are very happy to present this to you. I will tell you without your even opening it that it is a baby cup, and we intend to send it Outside to be inscribed with the following message...'Bestowed by grateful delegates upon an unborn child named Douthit who abided quietly throughout the Alaska Constitutional Convention and never offered an amendment.' "

Now the final moment had come. E. B. Collins, speaker of the House in that long-ago First Territorial Legislature, offered a few remarks. Recalling the first session of that first legislature, he said, "We wound up our duties with the same emotional scene as I have experienced here today. In that legislature, we formed a friendship that was enduring...and I can see here today that the association and the friendship...within this convention...will endure for time to come when we enjoy the statehood of Alaska." Then Collins requested that Mildred Hermann be given the privilege of offering the adjournment motion and Egan acceded.

"...I move when we go forth from this assembly today," said Mrs. Hermann, "we do so in memory of two great Alaskans who pioneered the statehood movement—Judge James Wickersham and Judge Anthony J. Dimond. Mr. President, I now move that we adjourn *sine die*."

Calling the roll for the last time, chief clerk Katherine Alexander was "barely able to pronounce the names through her tears."[5] The motion carried unanimously and the delegates rose to applaud the moment and one another.

Afterwards, in an informal session, the delegates at the suggestion of George Sundborg formed the Fifty-five Club to provide for reunions of the group. "It is inconceivable to think that we could ever really adjourn," Sundborg said.

Commented Burke Riley: "When the convention opened, no one knew what to expect or how much to hope for. Now we all know. The high purpose of the proceedings brought the best out in everyone. Now the convention is a known quantity. And no one wants it to end."[6]

23
Winning the Fight

THE CONSTITUTIONAL CONVENTION of 1955-56 had the hoped-for effect of stimulating a new national interest in Alaska's statehood quest and set in motion the final campaign for statehood. Political scientists and major newspapers and other periodicals saw the 14,400-word constitution itself as a concise, flexible plan, a distillation of the best from America's 180 years of experience in self-government.

"...Certainly the deliberations of this convention and its results speak well for the common sense and civic devotion of the delegates..." editorialized *The New York Times*, whose West Coast bureau chief covered part of the convention. "Its atmosphere was that of a pioneer America. These men and a few women...spoke the authentic American language." Taking a firm stand for statehood, the newspaper declared that "the present situation [of Alaskans] would be ridiculous if it were not so unjust."[1]

In the Territory, a bipartisan effort was launched to win ratification of the constitution and ordinances. Operation Statehood, the citizens' action group, played a significant role in this effort. The Alaska Statehood Committee on recommendation of the convention's Ratification Committee saw to the printing and distribution of 15,000 copies of the constitution and 100,000 pamphlets summarizing it.[2] The statehood committee also arranged for the printing—by the *Fairbanks Daily News-Miner*—of 50,000 copies of a special eight-page section on the work of the convention, including the full text of the constitution, which became supplements in all Alaska newspapers.[3] The committee sponsored radio and television programs on the constitution and a "Know Your Constitution" series of articles written by individual convention delegates for use by newspapers.[4]

Taxation Without Representation

FAIRBANKS, April 4, 1956—(AP)—A federal court jury...last night freed an Alaskan who had pleaded not guilty to...income tax evasion on grounds that he did not believe in "taxation without representation."

Jack Marler...was found innocent of charges that he willfully failed to file income tax returns...

...The defendant's attorney, Edgar Paul Boyko of Anchorage, announced before the trial that he would make the case "a test of the income tax laws as applied to the Territory of Alaska."

...In his instruction, the judge [U.S. District Judge Vernon D. Forbes] had told the jurors that the defense of "taxation without representation" was not valid, but the jury could take this defense into account in determining whether or not Marler had willfully failed to file his returns...

...U.S. Attorney Ted Stevens said he did not believe that this case was in any way a test of the federal income tax laws as applied to Alaska. . . .

WASHINGTON, April 19, 1956—(AP)—An Internal Revenue Service spokesman today shattered any dreams Alaskans might hold that a recent Fairbanks jury verdict might relieve them from federal tax responsibility.

...[The spokesman said]...the case..."establishes no precedent. . . . In this particular case the jury found for the taxpayer. In their opinion, his failure to file was not willful. That and nothing more. He [Jack Marler] must pay taxes for all the years he failed to file or pay..."

The delegates at every opportunity urged their fellow Alaskans to vote affirmatively and arranged for William Egan to stump the Territory for ten days on behalf of the constitution just before the April 24 ratification election. In his *Anchorage Daily Times* on April 20, statehood committee chairman Robert Atwood exhorted Alaskans to go to the polls and "tell the world they still want immediate statehood. Our stateside friends are waiting to hear how loud that voice will be. . . . Let's make it a clear, clarion call for Statehood Now." Other leaders in the statehood movement were similarly equating a vote for the constitution with a vote for statehood.

In the election, the vote was 17,447 for, 8,180 against, adoption of the constitution. This better than two-to-one margin prevailed in three of the four regions of the Territory. In Southeastern Alaska the vote was less enthusiastic: 4,163 for adoption, 3,397 against.

The Alaska-Tennessee Plan ordinance, providing for a full-time lobbying effort in Washington for statehood, was disapproved 3,920 to 3,252 in Southeastern Alaska but approved in the other three regions by more than two to one. The total vote was 15,011 for adoption, 9,556 against.[5] Alaskans everywhere voted overwhelmingly—21,185 to 4,004—to adopt the ordinance that would eliminate fish traps.

At their convention in June, Alaska Republicans nominated an Alaska-Tennessee Plan delegation including Robert Atwood and Territorial Senator John Butrovich of Fairbanks, who would run for the U.S. Senate, and retired U.S. Forest Service official Charles G. Burdick of Juneau, for the U.S. House of Representatives. The Democrats, convening the same month, nominated William Egan and Ernest Gruening for the Senate and Ralph Rivers for the House.

In the 1956 general election, held in October in Alaska, the Democrats captured all three seats. Only Gruening was pressed in the race. He defeated Butrovich 14,169 to 13,301. Egan outpolled Atwood 15,634 to 11,588, and Rivers defeated Burdick 15,569 to 11,345.

Shortly after the opening of the first session of the Eighty-fifth Congress in January 1957, Senator Spessard L. Holland of Florida, speaking for himself and Senator Russell Long of Louisiana, informed his Senate colleagues: "We are pleased and proud to advise the Senate that the people of Alaska held a constitutional convention last year and adopted a constitution, and likewise elected two senators and one representative to serve in the Congress of the United States when Alaska shall become a state of the Union, which I hope will be within the next few months." He was also "pleased to announce" that members of the Alaska-Tennessee Plan delegation, with their families, were seated in the Senate gallery, and he called on them to stand so the Senate could "extend to them a warm welcome."[6]

As the applause faded, Senator James E. Murray of Montana rose to compliment Alaskans "on their initiative in going ahead and drawing up a proposed state constitution and electing...provisional officers under it." He thought it was "highly significant and particularly gratifying...that while our fellow American citizens in Alaska have displayed such initiative, energy, and foresight...they have at the same time carefully stayed within the bounds of...precedent and tradition running back to the very beginnings of our Union of States."

Ten other senators, of both political parties, likewise rose to associate themselves with Holland on behalf of statehood. One of them, Joseph

C. O'Mahoney of Wyoming, concluded: "I cannot take my seat without complimenting Mr. Bartlett for the magnificent work he has done in and out of Congress to make statehood a reality for Alaska. . . ."

O'Mahoney was a little premature. Nearly a year and a half would elapse before a House-passed Alaska admission bill would be accepted and approved without change by the Senate, a period during which Bob Bartlett, the Alaska-Tennessee Plan delegation, Alaska Statehood Committee, Operation Statehood and individual Alaskans and others worked unceasingly to indeed make statehood a reality.

In the final stretch, the national administration finally came round on the Alaska statehood issue. In his budget message delivered at the opening of the Eighty-fifth Congress, President Eisenhower, beginning his second term, recommended the "enactment of legislation admitting Hawaii into the Union...and that subject to area limitations and other safeguards for the conduct of defense activities. . . . statehood also be conferred upon Alaska." While conditional, this presidential stance on Alaska statehood marked a turning point. Hereafter, the various federal agencies would cooperate closely with Congress in the drafting of statehood legislation, insisting only that lawmakers make provision for national defense land withdrawals in Alaska sought by the president.

Fred A. Seaton, who succeeded Douglas McKay as interior secretary in mid-1956, is widely credited for this turnaround. As a senator from Nebraska he had favored making Alaska a state and had not changed his mind on assuming the cabinet post. *Fairbanks Daily News-Miner* publisher C. W. Snedden, an acquaintance of Seaton, is said to have persuaded the interior secretary to press for Alaska statehood and recommended the employment of Ted Stevens, then U.S. attorney at Fairbanks, as his legislative counsel to assist with this effort. Stevens was duly retained by Seaton and worked aggressively in the cause.[7]

Snedden himself took up residence in Washington to take part in the roundup of congressional votes for statehood. Walter J. Hickel, as Republican national committeeman for Alaska, exerted his influence to keep the administration on track and pick up Republican votes in Congress. George Lehleitner was there too, speaking out for Alaska.

By 1957 the public had long approved of the statehood aspirations of Hawaii and Alaska. The Gallup polls for several years had indicated overwhelming sentiment for statehood.

There was good news and a little disappointing news for statehood supporters near the end of July 1957. The powerful House speaker, Sam Rayburn, formerly opposed to statehood, now decided to throw his weight behind it, but he advised the Alaska delegation that consideration of enabling legislation would have to wait until the opening of Congress in 1958. It could not be taken up in the hectic closing months of the 1957 session.[8]

The president in his 1958 budget message made only brief reference to the statehood question, recommending "that the Congress complete action on appropriate legislation admitting Hawaii and Alaska into the Union as states."

Representative Leo W. O'Brien of New York, wearing a shamrock tie clasp given him by Mrs. William (Neva) Egan for a little extra luck, led statehood forces to a 210-166 victory in the House on May 28. Senator Henry M. (Scoop) Jackson, floor manager for Alaska statehood legislation in the upper chamber, agreed to bring the House bill to a vote in the Senate without change, to maintain the momentum of the legislative drive.

The bill authorized the president to withdraw lands in northern and northwestern Alaska for national defense purposes, and it required Alaskans to approve the withdrawals as a condition of statehood. (This they would readily do, knowing that in a national emergency the president would be empowered to do whatever necessary for purposes of defense, including the taking of land. This provision of the bill has proved to be of no significance.)

Thunderous applause shook the Senate gallery the night of June 30, 1958, when the presiding officer, Senator Richard Neuberger, announced the Alaska statehood bill had carried sixty-four to twenty. Senators even applauded on the floor, which was against all rules, but statehood advocate Neuberger declined to wield his gavel.[9]

Celebrations erupted around the Territory when word flashed that statehood had been won. Civil defense and fire sirens blared and Alaskans rushed out onto the streets of the larger towns to acknowledge the historic moment. Some 25,000 Anchorage residents converged on the Park Strip in the evening for the biggest bonfire celebration in the city's history and the symbolic burning of the Organic Act under which the Territory was governed. A National Guard howitzer crew fired off forty-nine rounds and forty-nine civilian airplanes flew over the massive gathering. Fireworks cracked and flared late into the night. In Fairbanks, a huge gold star on a silken banner rose over the city, carried aloft by weather balloons which had been released from the roof of a downtown hotel. An attempt to dye the Chena River gold with packets of gold dye meant for use in air rescue attempts at sea went awry: the river, which curves through the heart of the city, turned bright green.

The Moment of Victory

"This is the greatest day in Alaska's history. The Congress has acted wisely and in the national interest. We of Alaska will justify what has been done this day."
—Delegate E. L. (Bob) Bartlett

"Thank God for everything that's happened here (in Washington). We will show the people of the United States they have not made a mistake."
—Territorial Governor Mike Stepovich

"It's the American tradition. We've seen it work today."
—Territorial Senator John Butrovich

"In this hour I cannot help but extend a grateful prayer of thanksgiving for the wonders of our American way of life and particularly in the wisdom of the Congress of the United States."
—Alaska-Tennessee Plan "Senator" William A. Egan

"I am confident [that] before long there will be few...who will not be wholly enthusiastic about the establishment of the 49th State."
—Alaska-Tennessee Plan "Senator" Ernest Gruening

(From an Associated Press story from Washington filed shortly after Senate passage of the statehood bill.)

President Eisenhower signed the statehood bill in private on July 7, setting the stage for the statehood elections and the resumption of all-out partisan politics.

In a special referendum conducted in conjunction with the August 26 primary election, Alaskans voted by margins of better than eight to one to accept statehood, the boundaries of the proposed state and other provisions of the statehood act.

In the fall, Interior Secretary Seaton and Vice President Richard Nixon campaigned vigorously in Alaska for the Republican candidates for statewide office—Territorial Senator John Butrovich, candidate for governor; Anchorage travel agency manager Brad Phillips, for secretary of state; former Territorial Governor Mike Stepovich of Fairbanks, who had succeeded B. Frank Heintzleman, and R. E. Robertson of Juneau, the delegate who departed the constitutional convention early, candidates for the U.S. Senate; and Henry A. Benson, former territorial labor commissioner, the U.S. House of Representatives. (Stepovich had resigned as the Territory's last appointed governor to run for the Senate.)

Another national figure, Senator John F. Kennedy of Massachusetts, came north to campaign for the Democratic candidates—William Egan, running for governor; Hugh J. Wade, former territorial treasurer, secretary of state; Ernest Gruening and Bob Bartlett, the U.S. Senate; and Ralph Rivers, for the U.S. House.

In the general election the Democrats triumphed, winning all the statewide offices and overwhelming control of the first state legislature.

A few minutes past noon on the third day of January 1959, a Saturday, President Eisenhower, with Nixon and House Speaker Rayburn beside him, signed the proclamation admitting Alaska to the Union as the forty-ninth state. Then he signed an executive order that would add a forty-ninth star to the nation's flag on the following Fourth of July. As press cameras banged and movie and television cameras whirred, the president unfurled a prototype of that flag with a forty-nine star field, seven staggered rows of seven stars each. Standing behind Eisenhower and looking on were Alaska's first congressional delegation—Bartlett, Gruening and Rivers—Seaton, Acting Territorial Governor Waino Hendrickson, Stepovich and Robert Atwood.

"Gentlemen," said the president to the assembled dignitaries and newsmen, "I think that all of us recognize this as an historic occasion. Certainly for myself I feel very privileged and honored to welcome the Forty-ninth State into the Union. Such a ceremony has not taken place in almost half a century, so at least I have the feeling of self-gratification that I am not just one of a group in this kind of ceremony.

"To the State itself, to its people, I extend on behalf of all their sister states, best wishes and hopes for prosperity and success. And to each of you gentlemen elected to high office to represent your new State...my congratulations, my felicitations, and my hope that we will all work together to the benefit of all forty-nine states. . . . "[10]

When Eisenhower strode into the White House Cabinet Room for the ceremony, it was nine in the morning and still dark in Juneau where, in the small antechamber off the governor's office on the third floor of the territorial capitol, Governor-elect Egan anxiously awaited word that the statehood proclamation had been signed. Some ten minutes later the news came over the Associated Press teletype in the second-floor press room, then the attorney general's office received word by telephone from Mary Lee Council, executive secretary to Senator-elect Bartlett, that statehood was a fact. Confirmation came from Eisenhower's press secretary, James Hagerty, and at nine-eighteen, as a clear, cold day dawned, Egan entered the governor's office and, with his wife Neva and eleven-year-old son Dennis and others witnessing the event, was sworn in as the first chief executive of the just-born State of Alaska.[11]

This historic day was devoid of the excitement that had swept Alaska five months earlier when a statehood bill had at last been enacted by Congress, when the outcome had been in doubt until the final roll call. But it was necessary to formalize Alaska's entry into the Union and now it was done.

Epilogue

JUST AS HE HAD BEEN THE RIGHT PERSON for the presidency of the constitutional convention, Bill Egan fit well in the governorship of the forty-ninth state. With a keen understanding of the state constitution and long familiarity with the workings of the legislature, he guided the new state with a sure hand during its formative years. He served three terms as governor. He was a strong, effective leader in the aftermath of the 1964 earthquake which devastated Southcentral Alaska, and he played an important part in the settlement of Native land claims in 1971. Back in private life he often spoke out on important public issues. He died in 1984 after a long battle with cancer.

Bob Bartlett too was well suited for his role as one of the state's first two U.S. senators. Well-known and respected in Congress, he moved rapidly and effectively to secure for Alaska those things to which it was entitled as a full-fledged member of the Union. Immensely popular, he was never threatened in his reelection campaigns. After a series of heart attacks, he died in 1968. (Ted Stevens, then a state legislator, was appointed by Governor Walter Hickel to fill the Senate vacancy and he continues to serve in that body.)

Well-known nationally, Ernest Gruening was a prominent and outspoken member of the U.S. Senate on Alaska and national issues. He and Wayne Morse of Oregon were the only senators to vote against adoption of the Tonkin Gulf resolution which opened the way for massive United States participation in the Vietnam War. After leaving office in 1968, he continued to speak out against the war. He died in 1974.

Bartlett and Gruening are a continuing presence in the national capitol. Bronze statues of them stand in Alaska's two places in Statuary Hall.

Alaska's first congressman, Ralph Rivers, effectively supported in the House the legislative efforts of Bartlett and Gruening on behalf of Alaska. He served four terms in the lower chamber and died in 1976.

Many of the constitutional convention delegates rose to prominence, chiefly as legislators, in the aftermath of the convention. Fifteen served in the twenty-third and last territorial legislature which met in 1957. There were fourteen in the first state legislature. Convention secretary Tom Stewart was also a member of that body, whose task it was to lay the legislative foundation for the state government. Delegates have served in all but two of the fifteen legislatures convened since statehood.

Warren Taylor was speaker of the House in the first and second state legislatures, Frank Peratrovich president of the Senate in the second and third, and Robert McNealy Senate president in the fourth state legislature.

The convention's chief clerk, Katherine Alexander (Hurley), of Wasilla, was Democratic nominee for lieutenant governor in 1978 and subsequently served a term in the House. She is a past president of the State Board of Education and former executive director of the Alaska Commission on the Status of Women.

Delegates also served the state in other ways.

Burke Riley was executive assistant to Governor Egan from 1959-61, assisting in the transition to statehood. He presently is a member of the Alaska Public Offices Commission. Following the convention, George Sundborg became editor of the *Fairbanks Daily News-Miner* and on Alaska's attainment of statehood was appointed administrative assistant to Senator Gruening, a position he held until Gruening left office.

Katherine Nordale was Juneau's postmaster for a number of years and Victor Fischer director of the University of Alaska's Institute of Social, Economic and Government Research and a state senator.

John Coghill, currently a state senator, was a special assistant to Governor Hickel and chairman of the Alaska Statehood Commission, created in 1980 to assess Alaska's progress since statehood. J. Rolland Armstrong was president of Sheldon Jackson College in Sitka for ten years.

Dorothy Awes (Haaland) has served as an assistant district attorney and assistant attorney general. Edward Davis, Seaborn Buckalew and Tom Stewart had long careers as superior court judges. Davis was one of the first judges appointed after statehood. Before his appointment to the bench, Buckalew was a legislator, district attorney and assistant adjutant general of the Alaska Air National Guard. Stewart had been administrative director of the Alaska court system before becoming a judge.

M. R. (Muktuk) Marston wrote of the organization and exploits of the Eskimo Scouts during the second world war in his 1969 book, *Men of the Tundra*, thereby keeping a promise to himself made years before to tell of the resourcefulness and courage of Alaska's Eskimo people.

George Lockwood, the Unalakleet Eskimo whose subsistence life style had been threatened by construction of a radar station on land he had long used, fondly recalls his friendship with Marston and Marston's efforts to obtain land for Alaska's Native people. "We as Natives, we owe him a lot. We loved him. He was really my friend." Lockwood, sixty-nine now, was compensated by the builders of the radar station for his loss of a fishing season. And he has the land he had long sought. Marston helped him to stake out a five-acre headquarters site many years ago which he has since converted to a 160-acre Native allotment. He and his wife Helen have nine children—eight living throughout Alaska and one in California—and a dozen grandchildren.

"An excellent constitution buttressed by the Tennessee Plan" won statehood for Alaska, says George Lehleitner, now living in retirement in Covington, Louisiana. The sending of an Alaska delegation to Washington was a dramatic event that "made news and brought new pressure on Congress, forcing it to act." The plan worked, he says, because it had bipartisan support. The first state legislature in 1959 recognized Lehleitner as the "father" of the Alaska-Tennessee Plan and on behalf of the people of Alaska thanked him "for his invaluable assistance in the successful bid for statehood." The Louisianan is also credited with having persuaded influential congressional leaders from his state to support Alaska statehood. With Alaska's admission to the Union, his work was done. The wall had been pulled down and Hawaii was quickly made the fiftieth state. Lehleitner contents himself now assisting the Salvation Army and promoting enrichment programs in local schools.

Florence Douthit, the reporter who covered the constitutional convention from beginning to end for the *Fairbanks Daily News-Miner*, gave birth to a daughter two months after its close in Yakima, Washington, where her husband had taken a reporting job. The second of four Douthit children, that daughter now resides in Oakland, California, is married and has a child of her own. A graduate of the University of California at Berkeley, she is a supervisor for a data processing firm. Florence Douthit returned to reporting for a time, in Berkeley, after her husband Jim joined the staff of the *Oakland Tribune*. She underwent lung cancer surgery in 1985, recovered, and the following year joined the cross-country peace march, walking more than 3,000 miles, from Los Angeles to Washington, D.C. In January 1988 she learned the cancer had recurred. She died four months later.

The fifty-five delegates to the Alaska Constitutional Convention were among those honored as "Founders of Alaska Statehood" at a formal dinner ceremony on the University of Alaska's Fairbanks campus on January 3, 1984, the twenty-fifth anniversary of statehood, proclaimed Alaska Statehood Day nationally and in the state. Far fewer than fifty-five were present to receive the special silver medals but all were remembered during the evening. Bill Egan, making one of his last public appearances, was there with his wife, Neva. Among others honored as founders of statehood were Bob Bartlett, Ernest Gruening and Anthony J. Dimond—honored posthumously—and George Lehleitner, Robert Atwood and Tom Stewart. The dinner was held in the massive campus center which dwarfs nearby Constitution Hall, a small building now but one which for seventy-five days in the winter of 1955-56 was the center of the campus—and Alaska.

Appendix 1

The Delegates, Their Hometowns and Occupations at Time of Convention

   R. Rolland Armstrong, Juneau, Presbyterian minister
   Dorothy J. Awes, Anchorage, attorney
* Frank Barr, Fairbanks, bush pilot
   John C. Boswell, Fairbanks, operations manager, U.S. Smelting, Refining and Mining Company
* Seaborn J. Buckalew, Anchorage, attorney
* John B. Coghill, Nenana, merchant
* Ernest B. Collins, Fairbanks, retired attorney
   George D. Cooper, Fairbanks, ready-mixed concrete plant owner
   John M. Cross, Kotzebue, commercial pilot
   Edward V. Davis, Anchorage, attorney
   James P. Doogan, Fairbanks, transfer company owner
* William A. Egan, Valdez, merchant
   Truman C. Emberg, Dillingham, business agent, Bristol Bay Fish Producers' Association
   Mrs. E. A. (Helen) Fischer, Anchorage, housewife
   Victor Fischer, Anchorage, planning consultant
   Douglas Gray, Douglas, hotel owner-operator
   Thomas C. Harris, Valdez, hotel manager, electronics engineer
   John S. Hellenthal, Anchorage, attorney
   Mildred R. Hermann, Juneau, attorney
   Herb Hilscher, Anchorage, public relations
   Jack Hinckel, Kodiak, petroleum products distributing firm owner-operator
   James Hurley, Palmer, general manager, Alaska Rural Rehabilitation Corporation
* Maurice T. Johnson, Fairbanks, attorney
   Yule F. Kilcher, Homer, homesteader, lecturer
   Leonard H. King, Haines, merchant
   William W. Knight, Sitka, merchant
* William W. Laws, Nome, retired police, fire chief
   Eldor R. Lee, Petersburg, fisherman, trapper
   Maynard D. Londborg, Unalakleet, missionary, Evangelical Mission, Covenant Church of America
* Steve McCutcheon, Anchorage, professional photographer

George M. McLaughlin, Anchorage, attorney
* Robert J. McNealy, Fairbanks, attorney
John A. McNees, Nome, beverage company owner
Marvin R. (Muktuk) Marston, Anchorage, real estate developer
Irwin L. Metcalf, Seward, grocery store owner-operator
Leslie Nerland, Fairbanks, retail furniture merchant
James Nolan, Wrangell, pharmacy owner
Katherine D. Nordale, Juneau, bank clerk
* Frank Peratrovich, Klawock, merchant
Chris Poulsen, Anchorage, theater owner
Peter L. Reader, Nome, gold dredge owner-operator
* Burke Riley, Haines, attorney
* Ralph J. Rivers, Fairbanks, attorney
* Victor C. Rivers, Anchorage, professional engineer
Ralph E. (Bob) Robertson, Juneau, attorney
John H. Rosswog, Cordova, merchant
Walter O. (Bo) Smith, Ketchikan, fisherman
Benjamin D. Stewart, Sitka, retired mining engineer
George W. Sundborg, Juneau, newspaper editor
* Dora M. Sweeney, Juneau, housewife
* Warren A. Taylor, Fairbanks, attorney
Herman R. (Van) VanderLeest, Juneau, retired pharmacist
* Michael J. Walsh, Nome, miner
Barrie M. White, Anchorage, newspaper dealer
Ada B. Wien, Fairbanks, housewife

* Served in legislature prior to convention

Appendix 2

THE CONSTITUTION of the STATE OF ALASKA

Ratified by the people of Alaska
April 24, 1956

Became operative with the formal
proclamation of statehood
January 3, 1959

Amended at various times since
proclamation of statehood

PREAMBLE

We the people of Alaska, grateful to God and to those who founded our nation and pioneered this great land, in order to secure and transmit to succeeding generations our heritage of political, civil, and religious liberty within the Union of States, do ordain and establish this constitution for the State of Alaska.

ARTICLE I
DECLARATION OF RIGHTS

Inherent Rights

SECTION 1. This constitution is dedicated to the principles that all persons have a natural right to life, liberty, the pursuit of happiness, and the enjoyment of the rewards of their own industry; that all persons are equal and entitled to equal rights, opportunities, and protection under the law; and that all persons have corresponding obligations to the people and to the State.

Source of Government

SECTION 2. All political power is inherent in the people. All government originates with the people, is founded upon their will only, and is instituted solely for the good of the people as a whole.

Civil Rights

SECTION 3. No person is to be denied the enjoyment of any civil or political right because of race, color, creed, sex, or national origin. The legislature shall implement this section.

(The amendment to this section was approved by the voters of the State August 22, 1972, and became effective October 14, 1972. It added the word "sex" to this section.)

Freedom of Religion

SECTION 4. No law shall be made respecting an establishment of religion, or prohibiting the free exercise thereof.

Freedom of Speech

SECTION 5. Every person may freely speak, write, and publish on all subjects, being responsible for the abuse of that right.

Assembly; Petition

SECTION 6. The right of the people peaceably to assemble, and to petition the government shall never be abridged.

Due Process

SECTION 7. No person shall be deprived of life, liberty, or property, without due process of law. The right of all persons to fair and just treatment in the course of legislative and executive investigations shall not be infringed.

Grand Jury

SECTION 8. No person shall be held to answer for a capital, or otherwise infamous crime, unless on a presentment or indictment of a grand jury, except in cases arising in the armed forces in time of war or public danger. Indictment may be waived by the accused. In that case the prosecution shall be by information. The grand jury shall consist of at least twelve citizens, a majority of whom concurring may return an indictment. The power of grand juries to investigate and make recommendations concerning the public welfare or safety shall never be suspended.

Jeopardy and Self-Incrimination

SECTION 9. No person shall be put in jeopardy twice for the same offense. No person shall be compelled in any criminal proceeding to be a witness against himself.

Treason

SECTION. 10. Treason against the State consists only in levying war against it, or in adhering to its enemies, giving them aid and comfort. No person shall be convicted of treason, unless on the testimony of two witnesses to the same overt act, or on confession in open court.

Rights of Accused	SECTION 11. In all criminal prosecutions, the accused shall have the right to a speedy and public trial, by an impartial jury of twelve, except that the legislature may provide for a jury of not more than twelve nor less than six in courts not of record. The accused is entitled to be informed of the nature and cause of the accusation; to be released on bail, except for capital offenses when the proof is evident or the presumption great; to be confronted with the witnesses against him; to have compulsory process for obtaining witnesses in his favor, and to have the assistance of counsel for his defense.
Excessive Punishment	SECTION 12. Excessive bail shall not be required, nor excessive fines imposed, nor cruel and unusual punishments inflicted. Penal administration shall be based on the principle of reformation and upon the need for protecting the public.
Habeas Corpus	SECTION 13. The privilege of the writ of habeas corpus shall not be suspended, unless when in cases of rebellion or actual or imminent invasion, the public safety requires it.
Searches and Seizures	SECTION 14. The right of the people to be secure in their persons, houses and other property, papers, and effects, against unreasonable searches and seizures, shall not be violated. No warrants shall issue, but upon probable cause, supported by oath or affirmation, and particularly describing the place to be searched, and the persons or things to be seized.
Prohibited State Action	SECTION 15. No bill of attainder or ex post facto law shall be passed. No law impairing the obligation of contracts, and no law making any irrevocable grant of special privileges or immunities shall be passed. No conviction shall work corruption of blood or forfeiture of estate.
Civil Suits; Trial by Jury	SECTION 16. In civil cases where the amount in controversy exceeds two hundred fifty dollars, the right of trial by a jury of twelve is preserved to the same extent as it existed at common law. The legislature may make provision for a verdict by not less than three-fourths of the jury and, in courts not of record, may provide for a jury of not less than six or more than twelve.
Imprisonment for Debt	SECTION 17. There shall be no imprisonment for debt. This section does not prohibit civil arrest of absconding debtors.
Eminent Domain	SECTION 18. Private property shall not be taken or damaged for public use without just compensation.
Right to Bear Arms	SECTION 19. A well-regulated militia being necessary to the security of a free state, the right of the people to keep and bear arms shall not be infringed.
Quartering Soldiers	SECTION 20. No member of the armed forces shall in time of peace be quartered in any house without the consent of the owner or occupant, or in time of war except as prescribed by law. The military shall be in strict subordination to the civil power.

Construction

SECTION 21. The enumeration of rights in this constitution shall not impair or deny others retained by the people.

Right of Privacy

SECTION 22. The right of the people to privacy is recognized and shall not be infringed. The legislature shall implement this section.

(The addition of this section, as an amendment to Article I, was approved by the voters of the State August 22, 1972, and became effective October 14, 1972.)

Resident Preference

SECTION 23. This constitution does not prohibit the State from granting preferences, on the basis of Alaska residence, to residents of the State over nonresidents to the extent permitted by the Constitution of the United States.

(The addition of this section, as an amendment to Article I, was approved by voters of the State November 8, 1988, and became effective thirty days after certification of the election.)

ARTICLE II
THE LEGISLATURE

Legislative Power; Membership

SECTION 1. The legislative power of the State is vested in a legislature consisting of a senate with a membership of twenty and a house of representatives with a membership of forty.

Members: Qualifications

SECTION 2. A member of the legislature shall be a qualified voter who has been a resident of Alaska for at least three years and of the district from which elected for at least one year, immediately preceding his filing for office. A senator shall be at least twenty-five years of age and a representative at least twenty-one years of age.

Election and Terms

SECTION 3. Legislators shall be elected at general elections. Their terms begin on the fourth Monday of the January following election unless otherwise provided by law. The term of representatives shall be two years, and the term of senators, four years. One-half of the senators shall be elected every two years.

(Exercising its authority under this section, the legislature has provided that terms begin on the second Monday in January, except in years immediately following a gubernatorial election when they begin on the third Monday in January.)

Vacancies

SECTION 4. A vacancy in the legislature shall be filled for the unexpired term as provided by law. If no provision is made, the governor shall fill the vacancy by appointment.

Disqualifications

SECTION 5. No legislator may hold any other office or position of profit under the United States or the State. During the term for which elected and for one year thereafter, no legislator may be nominated, elected, or appointed to any other office or position of profit which has been created, or the salary or emoluments of which have been increased, while he was a member. This section shall not prevent any person from seeking or holding the office of governor, lieutenant governor, or member of Congress. This section shall not apply to employment by or election to a constitutional convention.

Immunities

SECTION 6. Legislators may not be held to answer before any other tribunal for any statement made in the exercise of their legislative duties while the legislature is in session. Members attending, going to, or returning from legislative sessions are not subject to civil process and are privileged from arrest except for felony or breach of the peace.

Salary and Expenses

SECTION 7. Legislators shall receive annual salaries. They may receive a per diem allowance for expenses while in session and are entitled to travel expenses going to and from sessions. Presiding officers may receive additional compensation.

Regular Sessions

SECTION 8. The legislature shall convene in regular session each year on the fourth Monday in January, but the month and day may be changed by law. The legislature shall adjourn from regular session no later than one hundred twenty consecutive calendar days from the date it convenes except that a regular session may be extended once for up to ten consecutive calendar days. An extension of the regular session requires the affirmative vote of at least two-thirds of the membership of each house of the legislature. The legislature shall adopt as part of the uniform rules of procedure deadlines for scheduling session work not inconsistent with provisions controlling the length of the session.

(The amendment to this section was approved by the voters of the State November 6, 1984, and became effective December 30, 1984. It added all of the language after the first sentence, placing a limitation on the length of legislative sessions.)

Special Sessions

SECTION 9. Special sessions may be called by the governor or by vote of two-thirds of the legislators. The vote may be conducted by the legislative council or as prescribed by law. At special sessions called by the governor, legislation shall be limited to subjects designated in his proclamation calling the session, to subjects presented by him, and the reconsideration of bills vetoed by him after adjournment of the last regular session. Special sessions are limited to thirty days.

(The amendment to this section was approved by the voters of the State November 2, 1976, and became effective December 23, 1976. This amendment deleted "or" preceding "to subjects" in the third sentence and added "and the reconsideration of bills vetoed by him after adjournment of the last regular session.")

Adjournment

SECTION 10. Neither house may adjourn or recess for longer than three days unless the other concurs. If the two houses cannot agree on the time of adjournment and either house certifies the disagreement to the governor, he may adjourn the legislature.

Interim Committees

SECTION 11. There shall be a legislative council, and the legislature may establish other interim committees. The council and other interim committees may meet between legislative sessions. They may perform duties and employ personnel as provided by the legislature. Their members may receive an allowance for expenses while performing their duties.

Rules

SECTION 12. The houses of each legislature shall adopt uniform rules of procedure. Each house may choose its officers and employees. Each is the judge of the election and qualifications of its members and may expel a member with the concurrence of two-thirds of its members. Each shall keep a journal of its proceedings. A majority of the membership of each house constitutes a quorum to do business, but a smaller number may adjourn from day to day and may compel attendance of absent members. The legislature shall regulate lobbying.

Form of Bills

SECTION 13. Every bill shall be confined to one subject unless it is an appropriation bill or one codifying, revising, or rearranging existing laws. Bills for appropriations shall be confined to appropriations. The subject of each bill shall be expressed in the title. The enacting clause shall be: "Be it enacted by the Legislature of the State of Alaska."

Passage of Bills

SECTION 14. The legislature shall establish the procedure for enactment of bills into law. No bill may become law unless it has passed three readings in each house on three separate days, except that any bill may be advanced from second to third reading on the same day by concurrence of three-fourths of the house considering it. No bill may become law without an affirmative vote of a majority of the membership of each house. The yeas and nays on final passage shall be entered in the journal.

Veto

SECTION 15. The governor may veto bills passed by the legislature. He may, by veto, strike or reduce items in appropriation bills. He shall return any vetoed bill, with a statement of his objections, to the house of origin.

Action Upon Veto

SECTION 16. Upon receipt of a veto message during a regular session of the legislature, the legislature shall meet immediately in joint session and reconsider passage of the vetoed bill or item. Bills to raise revenue and appropriation bills or items, although vetoed, become law by affirmative vote of three-fourths of the membership of the legislature. Other vetoed bills become law by affirmative vote of two-thirds of the membership of the legislature. Bills vetoed after adjournment of the first regular session of the legislature shall be reconsidered by the legislature sitting as one body no later than the fifth day of the next regular or special session of that legislature. Bills vetoed after adjournment of the second regular session shall be reconsidered by the legislature sitting as one body no later than the fifth day of a special session of that legislature, if one is called. The vote on reconsideration of a vetoed bill shall be entered on the journals of both houses.

(The amendment to this section was approved by the voters of the State November 2, 1976, and became effective December 23, 1976. This amendment inserted "during a regular session of the legislature" in the first sentence and added the present fourth and fifth sentences.)

Bills Not Signed SECTION 17. A bill becomes law if, while the legislature is in session, the governor neither signs nor vetoes it within fifteen days, Sundays excepted, after its delivery to him. If the legislature is not in session and the governor neither signs nor vetoes a bill within twenty days, Sundays excepted, after its delivery to him, the bill becomes law.

Effective Date SECTION 18. Laws passed by the legislature become effective ninety days after enactment. The legislature may, by concurrence of two-thirds of the membership of each house, provide for another effective date.

Local or Special Acts SECTION 19. The legislature shall pass no local or special act if a general act can be made applicable. Whether a general act can be made applicable shall be subject to judicial determination. Local acts necessitating appropriations by a political subdivision may not become effective unless approved by a majority of the qualified voters voting thereon in the subdivision affected.

Impeachment SECTION 20. All civil officers of the State are subject to impeachment by the legislature. Impeachment shall originate in the senate and must be approved by a two-thirds vote of its members. The motion for impeachment shall list fully the basis for the proceeding. Trial on impeachment shall be conducted by the house of representatives. A supreme court justice designated by the court shall preside at the trial. Concurrence of two-thirds of the members of the house is required for a judgment of impeachment. The judgment may not extend beyond removal from office, but shall not prevent proceedings in the courts on the same or related charges.

Suits Against the State SECTION 21. The legislature shall establish procedures for suits against the State.

ARTICLE III
THE EXECUTIVE

Executive Power SECTION 1. The executive power of the State is vested in the governor.

Governor: **Qualifications**	SECTION 2. The governor shall be at least thirty years of age and a qualified voter of the State. He shall have been a resident of Alaska at least seven years immediately preceding his filing for office, and he shall have been a citizen of the United States for at least seven years.
Election	SECTION 3. The governor shall be chosen by the qualified voters of the State at a general election. The candidate receiving the greatest number of votes shall be governor.
Term of Office	SECTION 4. The term of office of the governor is four years, beginning at noon on the first Monday in December following his election and ending at noon on the first Monday in December four years later.
Limit on Tenure	SECTION 5. No person who has been elected governor for two full successive terms shall be again eligible to hold that office until one full term has intervened.
Dual Office Holding	SECTION 6. The governor shall not hold any other office or position of profit under the United States, the State, or its political subdivisions.
Lieutenant Governor: Duties	SECTION 7. There shall be a lieutenant governor. He shall have the same qualifications as the governor and serve for the same term. He shall perform such duties as may be prescribed by law and as may be delegated to him by the governor. (The amendment to this section was approved by the voters of the State August 25, 1970, and became effective October 10, 1970. The words "secretary of state" were changed to "lieutenant governor.")
Election	SECTION 8. The lieutenant governor shall be nominated in the manner provided by law for nominating candidates for other elective offices. In the general election the votes cast for a candidate for governor shall be considered as cast also for the candidate for lieutenant governor running jointly with him. The candidate whose name appears on the ballot jointly with that of the successful candidate for governor shall be elected lieutenant governor.
Acting Governor	SECTION 9. In case of the temporary absence of the governor from office, the lieutenant governor shall serve as acting governor.
Succession: Failure to Qualify	SECTION 10. If the governor-elect dies, resigns, or is disqualified, the lieutenant governor elected with him shall succeed to the office of governor for the full term. If the governor-elect fails to assume office for any other reason, the lieutenant governor elected with him shall serve as acting governor, and shall succeed to the office if the governor-elect does not assume his office within six months of the beginning of the term.
Vacancy	SECTION 11. In case of a vacancy in the office of governor for any reason, the lieutenant governor shall succeed to the office for the remainder of the term.

Absence	SECTION 12. Whenever for a period of six months, a governor has been continuously absent from office or has been unable to discharge the duties of his office by reason of mental or physical disability, the office shall be deemed vacant. The procedure for determining absence and disability shall be prescribed by law.
Further Succession	SECTION 13. Provisions shall be made by law for succession to the office of governor and for an acting governor in the event that the lieutenant governor is unable to succeed to the office or act as governor. No election of a lieutenant governor shall be held except at the time of electing a governor.
Title and Authority	SECTION 14. When the lieutenant governor succeeds to the office of governor, he shall have the title, powers, duties and emoluments of that office.
Compensation	SECTION 15. The compensation of the governor and the lieutenant governor shall be prescribed by law and shall not be diminished during their term of office, unless by general law applying to all salaried officers of the State.
Governor: Authority	SECTION 16. The governor shall be responsible for the faithful execution of the laws. He may, by appropriate court action or proceeding brought in the name of the State, enforce compliance with any constitutional or legislative mandate, or restrain violation of any constitutional or legislative power, duty, or right by any officer, department, or agency of the State or any of its political subdivisions. This authority shall not be construed to authorize any action or proceeding against the legislature.
Convening Legislature	SECTION 17. Whenever the governor considers it in the public interest, he may convene the legislature, either house, or the two houses in joint session.
Messages to Legislature	SECTION 18. The governor shall, at the beginning of each session, and may at other times, give the legislature information concerning the affairs of the State and recommend the measures he considers necessary.
Military Authority	SECTION 19. The governor is commander-in-chief of the armed forces of the State. He may call out these forces to execute the laws, suppress or prevent insurrection or lawless violence, or repel invasion. The governor, as provided by law, shall appoint all general and flag officers of the armed forces of the State, subject to confirmation by a majority of the members of the legislature in joint session. He shall appoint and commission all other officers.
Martial Law	SECTION 20. The governor may proclaim martial law when the public safety requires it in case of rebellion or actual or imminent invasion. Martial law shall not continue for longer than twenty days without the approval of a majority of the members of the legislature in joint session.

Executive Clemency	SECTION 21. Subject to procedure prescribed by law, the governor may grant pardons, commutations, and reprieves, and may suspend and remit fines and forfeitures. This power shall not extend to impeachment. A parole system shall be provided by law.
Executive Branch	SECTION 22. All executive and administrative offices, departments, and agencies of the state government and their respective functions, powers and duties shall be allocated by law among and within not more than twenty principal departments, so as to group them as far as practicable according to major purposes. Regulatory, quasi-judicial, and temporary agencies may be established by law and need not be allocated within a principal department.
Reorganization	SECTION 23. The governor may make changes in the organization of the executive branch or in the assignment of functions among its units which he considers necessary for efficient administration. Where these changes require the force of law, they shall be set forth in executive orders. The legislature shall have sixty days of a regular session, or a full session if of shorter duration, to disapprove these executive orders. Unless disapproved by resolution concurred in by a majority of the members in joint session, these orders become effective at a date thereafter to be designated by the governor.
Supervision	SECTION 24. Each principal department shall be under the supervision of the governor.
Department Heads	SECTION 25. The head of each principal department shall be a single executive unless otherwise provided by law. He shall be appointed by the governor, subject to confirmation by a majority of the members of the legislature in joint session, and shall serve at the pleasure of the governor, except as otherwise provided in this article with respect to the lieutenant governor. The heads of all principal departments shall be citizens of the United States.
Boards and Commissions	SECTION 26. When a board or commission is at the head of a principal department or a regulatory or quasi-judicial agency, its members shall be apppointed by the governor, subject to confirmation by a majority of the members of the legislature in joint session, and may be removed as provided by law. They shall be citizens of the United States. The board or commission may appoint a principal executive officer when authorized by law, but the appointment shall be subject to the approval of the governor.
Recess Appointments	SECTION 27. The governor may make appointments to fill vacancies occurring during a recess of the legislature, in offices requiring confirmation by the legislature. The duration of such appointments shall be prescribed by law.

ARTICLE IV
THE JUDICIARY

Judicial Power and Jurisdiction	SECTION 1. The judicial power of the State is vested in a supreme court, a superior court and the courts established by the legislature. The jurisdiction of courts shall be prescribed by law. The courts shall constitute a unified judicial system for operation and administration. Judicial districts shall be established by law.

Supreme Court

SECTION 2. (a) The supreme court shall be the highest court of the State, with final appellate jurisdiction. It shall consist of three justices, one of whom is chief justice. The number of justices may be increased by law upon the request of the supreme court.

(b) The chief justice shall be selected from among the justices of the supreme court by a majority vote of the justices. His term of office as chief justice is three years. A justice may serve more than one term as chief justice but he may not serve consecutive terms in that office.

(The amendment to this section was approved by the voters of the State August 25, 1970, and became effective October 10, 1970. It added subsection (b).)

Superior Court

SECTION 3. The superior court shall be the trial court of general jurisdiction and shall consist of five judges. The number of judges may be changed by law.

Qualifications of Justices and Judges

SECTION 4. Supreme court justices and superior court judges shall be citizens of the United States and of the State, licensed to practice law in the State, and possessing any additional qualifications prescribed by law. Judges of other courts shall be selected in a manner, for terms, and with qualifications prescribed by law.

Nomination and Appointment

SECTION 5. The governor shall fill any vacancy in an office of supreme court justice or superior court judge by appointing one of two or more persons nominated by the judicial council.

Approval or Rejection

SECTION 6. Each supreme court justice and superior court judge shall, in the manner provided by law, be subject to approval or rejection on a nonpartisan ballot at the first general election held more than three years after his appointment. Thereafter, each supreme court justice shall be subject to approval or rejection in a like manner every tenth year, and each superior court judge, every sixth year.

Vacancy

SECTION 7. The office of any supreme court justice or superior court judge becomes vacant ninety days after the election at which he is rejected by a majority of those voting on the question, or for which he fails to file his declaration of candidacy to succeed himself.

Judicial Council

SECTION 8. The judicial council shall consist of seven members. Three attorney members shall be appointed for six-year terms by the governing body of the organized state bar. Three non-attorney members shall be appointed for six-year terms by the governor subject to confirmation by a majority of the members of the legislature in joint session. Vacancies shall be filled for the unexpired term in like manner. Appointments shall be made with due consideration to area representation and without regard to political affiliation. The chief justice of the supreme court shall be ex officio the seventh member and chairman of the judicial council. No member of the judicial council, except the chief justice, may hold any other office or position of profit under the United States or the State. The judicial council shall act by concurrence of four or more members and according to rules which it adopts.

Additional Duties

SECTION 9. The judicial council shall conduct studies for improvement of the administration of justice, and make reports and recommendations to the supreme court and to the legislature at intervals of not more than two years. The judicial council shall perform other duties assigned by law.

Commission on Judicial Conduct

SECTION 10. The Commission on Judicial Conduct shall consist of nine members as follows: three persons who are justices or judges of state courts, elected by the justices and judges of state courts; three members who have practiced law in this state for ten years, appointed by the governor from nominations made by the governing body of the organized bar and subject to confirmation by a majority of the members of the legislature in joint session; and three persons who are not judges, retired judges, or members of the state bar, appointed by the governor and subject to confirmation by a majority of the members of the legislature in joint session. In addition to being subject to impeachment under Section 12 of this article, a justice or judge may be disqualified from acting as such and may be suspended, removed from office, retired, or censured by the supreme court upon the recommendation of the commission. The powers and duties of the commission and the bases for judicial disqualification shall be established by law.

(The addition of this section, as an amendment to Article IV, was approved by the voters of the State August 27, 1968, and became effective October 11, 1968. The section replaced the original section pertaining to incapacity of judges and provided for creation of a Commission on Judicial Qualifications. An amendment approved November 2, 1982, which became effective December 24, 1982, changed the name of the commission to the Commission on Judicial Conduct.)

Retirement

SECTION 11. Justices and judges shall be retired at the age of seventy except as provided in this article. The basis and amount of retirement pay shall be prescribed by law. Retired judges shall render no further service on the bench except for special assignments as provided by court rule.

Impeachment

SECTION 12. Impeachment of any justice or judge for malfeasance or misfeasance in the performance of his official duties shall be according to procedure prescribed for civil officers.

Compensation

SECTION 13. Justices, judges, and members of the judicial council and the Commission on Judicial Conduct shall receive compensation as prescribed by law. Compensation of justices and judges shall not be diminished during their terms of office, unless by general law applying to all salaried officers of the State.

Restrictions

SECTION 14. Supreme court justices and superior court judges while holding office may not practice law, hold office in a political party, or hold any other office or position of profit under the United States, and the State, or its political subdivisions. Any supreme court justice or superior court judge filing for another elective public office forfeits his judicial position.

Constitution / 119

Rule-making Power

SECTION 15. The supreme court shall make and promulgate rules governing the administration of all courts. It shall make and promulgate rules governing practice and procedure in civil and criminal cases in all courts. These rules may be changed by the legislature by two-thirds vote of the members elected to each house.

Court Administration

SECTION 16. The chief justice of the supreme court shall be the administrative head of all courts. He may assign judges from one court or division thereof to another for temporary service. The chief justice shall, with the approval of the supreme court, appoint an administrative director to serve at the pleasure of the supreme court and to supervise the administrative operations of the judicial system.

(The amendment to this section was approved by the voters of the State August 25, 1970, and became effective October 10, 1970. It substituted "the pleasure of the supreme court" for "his pleasure" in the last sentence.)

ARTICLE V
SUFFRAGE AND ELECTIONS

Qualified Voters

SECTION 1. Every citizen of the United States who is at least eighteen years of age, who meets registration residency requirements which may be prescribed by law, and who is qualified to vote under this article, may vote in any state or local election. A voter shall have been, immediately preceding the election, a thirty-day resident of the election district in which he seeks to vote, except that for purposes of voting for President and Vice President of the United States other residency requirements may be prescribed by law. Additional voting qualifications may be prescribed by law for bond issue elections of political subdivisions.

(The first two amendments to this section were approved by the voters August 23, 1966, and became effective October 9, 1966. They substituted "a voter" for "He" at the beginning of the second sentence and provided that separate residency requirements for presidential elections could be prescribed by law. The third amendment, approved August 25, 1970, and effective October 10, 1970, changed the voting age from 19 to 18 years. The fourth amendment, approved August 25, 1970, and effective October 10, 1970, deleted the sentence "A voter shall be able to read or speak the English language as prescribed by law, unless prevented by physical disability." The fifth amendment, approved August 22, 1972, and effective October 14, 1972, inserted "residency" in the first sentence and deleted the requirement of one year's residence in Alaska which appeared in the second sentence.)

Disqualification

SECTION 2. No person may vote who has been convicted of a felony involving moral turpitude unless his civil rights have been restored. No person may vote who has been judicially determined to be of unsound mind unless the disability has been removed.

Methods of Voting; Election Contests	SECTION 3. Methods of voting, including absentee voting, shall be prescribed by law. Secrecy of voting shall be preserved. The procedure for determining election contests, with right of appeal to the courts, shall be prescribed by law.
Voting Precincts; Registration	SECTION 4. The legislature may provide a system of permanent registration of voters, and may establish voting precincts within election districts.
General Elections	SECTION 5. General elections shall be held on the second Tuesday in October of every even-numbered year, but the month and day may be changed by law.
	(Exercising its authority under this section, the legislature has provided that the date of the general election is the Tuesday after the first Monday in November in every even-numbered year.)

ARTICLE VI
LEGISLATIVE APPORTIONMENT

Election Districts	SECTION 1. Members of the house of representatives shall be elected by the qualified voters of the respective election districts. Until reapportionment, election districts and the number of representatives to be elected from each district shall be as set forth in Section 1 of Article XIV.
Senate Districts	SECTION 2. Members of the senate shall be elected by the qualified voters of the respective senate districts. Senate districts shall be as set forth in Section 2 of Article XIV, subject to changes authorized in this article.
Reapportionment of House	SECTION 3. The governor shall reapportion the house of representatives immediately following the official reporting of each decennial census of the United States. Reapportionment shall be based upon civilian population within each election district as reported by the census.
Method	SECTION 4. Reapportionment shall be by the method of equal proportions, except that each election district having the major fraction of the quotient obtained by dividing total civilian population by forty shall have one representative.
Combining Districts	SECTION 5. Should the total civilian population within any election district fall below one-half of the quotient, the district shall be attached to an election district within its senate district, and the reapportionment for the new district shall be determined as provided in Section 4 of this article.
Redistricting	SECTION 6. The governor may further redistrict by changing the size and area of election districts, subject to the limitations of this article. Each new district so created shall be formed of contiguous and compact territory containing as nearly as practicable a relatively integrated socio-economic area. Each shall contain a population at least equal to the quotient obtained by dividing the total civilian population by forty. Consideration may be given to local government boundaries. Drainage and other geographic features shall be used in describing boundaries wherever possible.

Modification of Senate Districts

SECTION 7. The senate districts, described in Section 2 of Article XIV, may be modified to reflect changes in election districts. A district, although modified, shall retain its total number of senators and its approximate perimeter.

Reapportionment Board

SECTION 8. The governor shall appoint a reapportionment board to act in an advisory capacity to him. It shall consist of five members, none of whom may be public employees or officials. At least one member each shall be appointed from the Southeastern, Southcentral, Central and Northwestern senate districts. Appointments shall be made without regard to political affiliation. Board members shall be compensated.

Organization

SECTION 9. The board shall elect one of its members chairman and may employ temporary assistants. Concurrence of three members is required for a ruling or determination, but a lesser number may conduct hearings or otherwise act for the board.

Reapportionment Plan and Proclamation

SECTION 10. Within ninety days following the official reporting of each decennial census, the board shall submit to the governor a plan for reapportionment and redistricting as provided in this article. Within ninety days after receipt of the plan, the governor shall issue a proclamation of reapportionment and redistricting. An accompanying statement shall explain any change from the plan of the board. The reapportionment and redistricting shall be effective for the election of members of the legislature until after the official reporting of the next decennial census.

Enforcement

SECTION 11. Any qualified voter may apply to the superior court to compel the governor, by mandamus or otherwise, to perform his reapportionment duties or to correct any error in redistricting or reapportionment. Application to compel the governor to perform his reapportionment duties must be filed within thirty days of the expiration of either of the two ninety-day periods specified in this article. Application to compel correction of any error in redistricting or reapportionment must be filed within thirty days following the proclamation. Original jurisdiction in these matters is hereby vested in the superior court. On appeal, the cause shall be reviewed by the supreme court upon the law and the facts.

ARTICLE VII
HEALTH, EDUCATION, AND WELFARE

Public Education

SECTION 1. The legislature shall by general law establish and maintain a system of public schools open to all children of the State, and may provide for other public educational institutions. Schools and institutions so established shall be free from sectarian control. No money shall be paid from public funds for the direct benefit of any religious or other private educational institution.

State University

SECTION 2. The University of Alaska is hereby established as the state university and constituted a body corporate. It shall have title to all real and personal property now or hereafter set aside for or conveyed to it. Its property shall be administered and disposed of according to law.

Board of Regents	SECTION 3. The University of Alaska shall be governed by a board of regents. The regents shall be appointed by the governor, subject to confirmation by a majority of the members of the legislature in joint session. The board shall, in accordance with law, formulate policy and appoint the president of the university. He shall be the executive officer of the board.
Public Health	SECTION 4. The legislature shall provide for the promotion and protection of public health.
Public Welfare	SECTION 5. The legislature shall provide for public welfare.

ARTICLE VIII
NATURAL RESOURCES

Statement of Policy	SECTION 1. It is the policy of the State to encourage the settlement of its land and the development of its resources by making them available for maximum use consistent with the public interest.
General Authority	SECTION 2. The legislature shall provide for the utilization, development, and conservation of all natural resources belonging to the State, including land and waters, for the maximum benefit of its people.
Common Use	SECTION 3. Wherever occurring in the natural state, fish, wildlife, and waters are reserved to the people for common use.
Sustained Yield	SECTION 4. Fish, forests, wildlife, grasslands, and all other replenishable resources belonging to the State shall be utilized, developed, and maintained on the sustained yield principle, subject to preferences among beneficial uses.
Facilities and Improvements	SECTION 5. The legislature may provide for facilities, improvements, and services to assure greater utilization, development, reclamation, and settlement of lands, and to assure fuller utilization and development of the fisheries, wildlife, and waters.
State Public Domain	SECTION 6. Lands and interests therein, including submerged and tidal lands, possessed or acquired by the State, and not used or intended exclusively for governmental purposes, constitute the state public domain. The legislature shall provide for the selection of lands granted to the State by the United States, and for the administration of the state public domain.
Special Purpose Sites	SECTION 7. The legislature may provide for the acquisition of sites, objects, and areas of natural beauty or of historic, cultural, recreational, or scientific value. It may reserve them from the public domain and provide for their administration and preservation for the use, enjoyment, and welfare of the people.
Leases	SECTION 8. The legislature may provide for the leasing of, and the issuance of permits for exploration of, any part of the public domain or interest therein, subject to reasonable concurrent uses. Leases and permits shall provide, among other conditions, for payment by the party at fault for damage or injury arising from noncompliance with terms governing concurrent use, and for forfeiture in the event of breach of conditions.

Sales and Grants	SECTION 9. Subject to the provisions of this section, the legislature may provide for the sale or grant of state lands, or interests therein, and establish sales procedures. All sales or grants shall contain such reservations to the State of all resources as may be required by Congress or the State and shall provide for access to these resources. Reservation of access shall not unnecessarily impair the owners' use, prevent the control of trespass, or preclude compensation for damages.
Public Notice	SECTION 10. No disposals or leases of state lands, or interests therein, shall be made without prior public notice and other safeguards of the public interest as may be prescribed by law.
Mineral Rights	SECTION 11. Discovery and appropriation shall be the basis for establishing a right in those minerals reserved to the State which, upon the date of ratification of this constitution by the people of Alaska, were subject to location under the federal mining laws. Prior discovery, location, and filing, as prescribed by law, shall establish a prior right to these minerals and also a prior right to permits, leases, and transferable licenses for their extraction. Continuation of these rights shall depend upon the performance of annual labor, or the payment of fees, rents, or royalties, or upon other requirements as may be prescribed by law. Surface uses of land by a mineral claimant shall be limited to those necessary for the extraction or basic processing of the mineral deposits, or for both. Discovery and appropriation shall initiate a right, subject to further requirements of law, to patent of mineral lands if authorized by the State and not prohibited by Congress. The provisions of this section shall apply to all other minerals reserved to the State which by law are declared subject to appropriation.
Mineral Leases and Permits	SECTION 12. The legislature shall provide for the issuance, types and terms of leases for coal, oil, gas, oil shale, sodium, phosphate, potash, sulfur, pumice, and other minerals as may be prescribed by law. Leases and permits giving the exclusive right of exploration for these minerals for specific periods and areas, subject to reasonable concurrent exploration as to different classes of minerals, may be authorized by law. Like leases and permits giving the exclusive right or prospecting by geophysical, geochemical, and similar methods for all minerals may also be authorized by law.
Water Rights	SECTION 13. All surface and subsurface waters reserved to the people for common use, except mineral and medicinal waters, are subject to appropriation. Priority of appropriation shall give prior right. Except for public water supply, an appropriation of water shall be limited to stated purposes and subject to preferences among beneficial uses, concurrent or otherwise, as prescribed by law, and to the general reservation of fish and wildlife.
Access to Navigable Waters	SECTION 14. Free access to the navigable or public waters of the State, as defined by the legislature, shall not be denied any citizen of the United States or resident of the State, except that the legislature may by general law regulate and limit such access for other beneficial uses or public purposes.

No Exclusive Right of Fishery	SECTION 15. No exclusive right or special privilege of fishery shall be created or authorized in the natural waters of the State. This section does not restrict the power of the State to limit entry into any fishery for purposes of resource conservation, to prevent economic distress among fishermen and those dependent upon them for a livelihood and to promote the efficient development of aquaculture in the State.
	(The amendment to this section was approved by the voters of the State August 22, 1972, and became effective October 14, 1972. This amendment added the second sentence.)
Protection of Rights	SECTION 16. No person shall be involuntarily divested of his right to the use of waters, his interests in lands, or improvements affecting either, except for a superior beneficial use or public purpose and then only with just compensation and by operation of law.
Uniform Application	SECTION 17. Laws and regulations governing the use or disposal of natural resources shall apply equally to all persons similarly situated with reference to the subject matter and purpose to be served by the law or regulation.
Private Ways of Necessity	SECTION 18. Proceeding in eminent domain may be undertaken for private ways of necessity to permit essential access for extraction or utilization of resources. Just compensation shall be made for property taken or for resultant damages to other property rights.

ARTICLE IX
FINANCE AND TAXATION

Taxing Power	SECTION 1. The power of taxation shall never be surrendered. This power shall not be suspended or contracted away, except as provided in this article.
Non-discrimination	SECTION 2. The lands and other property belonging to citizens of the United States residing without the State shall never be taxed at a higher rate than the lands and other property belonging to the residents of the State.
Assessment Standards	SECTION 3. Standards for appraisal of all property assessed by the State or its political subdivisions shall be prescribed by law.
Exemptions	SECTION 4. The real and personal property of the State or its political subdivisions shall be exempt from taxation under conditions and exceptions which may be provided by law. All, or any portion of, property used exclusively for nonprofit religious, charitable, cemetery, or educational purposes, as defined by law, shall be exempt from taxation. Other exemptions of like or different kind may be granted by general law. All valid existing exemptions shall be retained until otherwise provided by law.
Interests in Government Property	SECTION 5. Private leaseholds, contracts, or interests in land or property owned or held by the United States, the State, or its political subdivisions, shall be taxable to the extent of the interests.

Public Purpose

SECTION 6. No tax shall be levied, or appropriation of public money made, or public property transferred, nor shall the public credit be used, except for a public purpose.

Dedicated Funds

SECTION 7. The proceeds of any state tax or license shall not be dedicated to any special purpose, except as provided in Section 15 of this article or when required by the federal government for state participation in federal programs. This provision shall not prohibit the continuance of any dedication for special purposes existing upon the date of ratification of this section by the people of Alaska.

(The amendment to this section was approved by the voters of the State November 2, 1976, and became effective February 21, 1977. This amendment inserted "as provided in Section 15 of this article or" in the first sentence.)

State Debt

SECTION 8. No state debt shall be contracted unless authorized by law for capital improvements or unless authorized by law for housing loans for veterans, and ratified by a majority of the qualified voters of the State who vote on the question. The State may, as provided by law and without ratification, contract debt for the purpose of repelling invasion, suppressing insurrection, defending the State in war, meeting natural disasters, or redeeming indebtedness outstanding at the time this constitution becomes effective.

(The amendment to this section, approved by the voters November 2, 1982, and effective December 24, 1982, inserted "or unless authorized by law for housing loans for veterans" in the first sentence.)

Local Debts

SECTION 9. No debt shall be contracted by any political subdivision of the State, unless authorized for capital improvements by its governing body and ratified by a majority vote of those qualified to vote and voting on the question.

Interim Borrowing

SECTION 10. The State and its political subdivisions may borrow money to meet appropriations for any fiscal year in anticipation of the collection of the revenues for that year, but all debt so contracted shall be paid before the end of the next fiscal year.

Exceptions

SECTION 11. The restrictions on contracting debt do not apply to debt incurred through the issuance of revenue bonds by a public enterprise or public corporation of the State or a political subdivision, when the only security is the revenues of the enterprise or corporation. The restrictions do not apply to indebtedness to be paid from special assessments on the benefited property, nor do they apply to refunding indebtedness of the State or its political subdivisions.

Budget

SECTION 12. The governor shall submit to the legislature, at a time fixed by law, a budget for the next fiscal year setting forth all proposed expenditures and anticipated income of all departments, offices, and agencies of the State. The governor, at the same time, shall submit a general appropriation bill to authorize the proposed expenditures, and a bill or bills covering recommendations in the budget for new or additional revenues.

Expenditures

SECTION 13. No money shall be withdrawn from the treasury except in accordance with appropriations made by law. No obligation for the payment of money shall be incurred except as authorized by law. Unobligated appropriations outstanding at the end of the period of time specified by law shall be void.

Legislative Post-Audit

SECTION 14. The legislature shall appoint an auditor to serve at its pleasure. He shall be a certified public accountant. The auditor shall conduct post-audits as prescribed by law and shall report to the legislature and to the governor.

Alaska Permanent Fund

SECTION 15. At least twenty-five percent of all mineral lease rentals, royalties, royalty sale proceeds, federal mineral revenue-sharing payments and bonuses received by the State shall be placed in a permanent fund, the principal of which shall be used only for those income-producing investments specifically designated by law as eligible for permanent fund investments. All income from the permanent fund shall be deposited in the general fund unless otherwise provided by law.

(The addition of this section was approved by the voters of the State November 2, 1976, and became effective February 21, 1977.)

Appropriation Limit

SECTION 16. Except for appropriations for Alaska permanent fund dividends, appropriations of revenue bond proceeds, appropriations required to pay the principal and interest on general obligation bonds, and appropriations of money received from a non-state source in trust for a specific purpose, including revenues of a public enterprise or public corporation of the State that issues revenue bonds, appropriations from the treasury made for a fiscal year shall not exceed $2,500,000,000 by more than the cumulative change, derived from federal indices as prescribed by law, in population and inflation since July 1, 1981. Within this limit, at least one-third shall be reserved for capital projects and loan appropriations. The legislature may exceed this limit in bills for appropriations to the Alaska permanent fund and in bills for appropriations for capital projects, whether of bond proceeds or otherwise, if each bill is approved by the governor, or passed by affirmative vote of three-fourths of the membership of the legislature over a veto or item veto, or becomes law without signature, and is also approved by the voters as prescribed by law. Each bill for appropriations for capital projects in excess of the limit shall be confined to capital projects of the same type, and the voters shall, as provided by law, be informed of the cost of operations and maintenance of the capital projects. No other appropriation in excess of this limit may be made except to meet a state of disaster declared by the governor as prescribed by law. The governor shall cause any unexpended and unappropriated balance to be invested so as to yield competitive market rates to the treasury.

(The addition of this section, as an amendment to Article IX, was approved by the voters of the State November 2, 1982, and became effective December 24, 1982.)

ARTICLE X
LOCAL GOVERNMENT

Purpose and Construction

SECTION 1. The purpose of this article is to provide for maximum local self-government with a minimum of local government units, and to prevent duplication of tax-levying jurisdictions. A liberal construction shall be given to the powers of local government units.

Local Government Powers

SECTION 2. All local government powers shall be vested in boroughs and cities. The State may delegate taxing powers to organized boroughs and cities only.

Boroughs

SECTION 3. The entire State shall be divided into boroughs, organized or unorganized. They shall be established in a manner and according to standards provided by law. The standards shall include population, geography, economy, transportation, and other factors. Each borough shall embrace an area and population with common interests to the maximum degree possible. The legislature shall classify boroughs and prescribe their powers and functions. Methods by which boroughs may be organized, incorporated, merged, consolidated, reclassified, or dissolved shall be prescribed by law.

Assembly

SECTION 4. The governing body of the organized borough shall be the assembly, and its composition shall be established by law or charter.

(The amendment to this section was approved by the voters of the State August 22, 1972, and became effective October 14, 1972. It deleted the second and third sentences which provided for city and non-city representation on the borough assembly.)

Service Areas

SECTION 5. Service areas to provide special services within an organized borough may be established, altered, or abolished by the assembly, subject to the provisions of law or charter. A new service area shall not be established if, consistent with the purposes of this article, the new service can be provided by an existing service area, by incorporation as a city, or by annexation to a city. The assembly may authorize the levying of taxes, charges, or assessments within a service area to finance the special services.

Unorganized Boroughs

SECTION 6. The legislature shall provide for the performance of services it deems necessary or advisable in unorganized boroughs, allowing for maximum local participation and responsibility. It may exercise any power or function in an unorganized borough which the assembly may exercise in an organized borough.

Cities

SECTION 7. Cities shall be incorporated in a manner prescribed by law, and shall be a part of the borough in which they are located. Cities shall have the powers and functions conferred by law or charter. They may be merged, consolidated, classified, reclassified, or dissolved in the manner provided by law.

Council

SECTION 8. The governing body of a city shall be the council.

Charters

SECTION 9. The qualified voters of any borough of the first class or city of the first class may adopt, amend, or repeal a home rule charter in a manner provided by law. In the absence of such legislation, the governing body of a borough or city of the first class shall provide the procedure for the preparation and adoption or rejection of the charter. All charters, or parts or amendments of charters, shall be submitted to the qualified voters of the borough or city, and shall become effective if approved by a majority of those who vote on the specific question.

Extended Home Rule

SECTION 10. The legislature may extend home rule to other boroughs and cities.

Home Rule Powers

SECTION 11. A home rule borough or city may exercise all legislative powers not prohibited by law or by charter.

Boundaries

SECTION 12. A local boundary commission or board shall be established by law in the executive branch of the state government. The commission or board may consider any proposed local government boundary change. It may present proposed changes to the legislature during the first ten days of any regular session. The change shall become effective forty-five days after presentation or at the end of the session, whichever is earlier, unless disapproved by a resolution concurred in by a majority of the members of each house. The commission or board, subject to law, may establish procedures whereby boundaries may be adjusted by local action.

Agreements; Transfer of Powers

SECTION 13. Agreements, including those for cooperative or joint administration of any functions or powers, may be made by any local government with any other local government, with the State, or with the United States, unless otherwise provided by law or charter. A city may transfer to the borough in which it is located any of its powers or functions unless prohibited by law or charter, and may in like manner revoke the transfer.

Local Government Agency

SECTION 14. An agency shall be established by law in the executive branch of the state government to advise and assist local governments. It shall review their activities, collect and publish local government information, and perform other duties prescribed by law.

Special Service Districts

SECTION 15. Special service districts existing at the time a borough is organized shall be integrated with the government of the borough as provided by law.

ARTICLE XI
INITIATIVE, REFERENDUM, AND RECALL

Initiative and Referendum

SECTION 1. The people may propose and enact laws by the initiative, and approve or reject acts of the legislature by the referendum.

Application	SECTION 2. An initiative or referendum is proposed by an application containing the bill to be initiated or the act to be referred. The application shall be signed by not less than one hundred qualified voters as sponsors, and shall be filed with the lieutenant governor. If he finds it in proper form he shall so certify. Denial of certification shall be subject to judicial review.
Petition	SECTION 3. After certification of the application, a petition containing a summary of the subject matter shall be prepared by the lieutenant governor for circulation by the sponsors. If signed by qualified voters, equal in number to ten per cent of those who voted in the preceding general election and resident in at least two-thirds of the election districts of the State, it may be filed with the lieutenant governor.
Initiative Election	SECTION 4. An initiative petition may be filed at any time. The lieutenant governor shall prepare a ballot title and proposition summarizing the proposed law, and shall place them on the ballot for the first statewide election held more than one hundred twenty days after adjournment of the legislative session following the filing. If, before the election, substantially the same measure has been enacted, the petition is void.
Referendum Election	SECTION 5. A referendum petition may be filed only within ninety days after adjournment of the legislative session at which the act was passed. The lieutenant governor shall prepare a ballot title and proposition summarizing the act and shall place them on the ballot for the first statewide election held more than one hundred eighty days after adjournment of that session.
Enactment	SECTION 6. If a majority of the votes cast on the proposition favor its adoption, the initiated measure is enacted. If a majority of the votes cast on the proposition favor the rejection of an act referred, it is rejected. The lieutenant governor shall certify the election returns. An initiated law becomes effective ninety days after certification, is not subject to veto, and may not be repealed by the legislature within two years of its effective date. It may be amended at any time. An act rejected by referendum is void thirty days after certification. Additional procedures for the initiative and the referendum may be prescribed by law.
Restrictions	SECTION 7. The initiative shall not be used to dedicate revenues, make or repeal appropriations, create courts, define the jurisdiction of courts or prescribe their rules, or enact local or special legislation. The referendum shall not be applied to dedications of revenue, to appropriations, to local or special legislation, or to laws necessary for the immediate preservation of the public peace, health, or safety.
Recall	SECTION 8. All elected public officials in the State, except judicial officers, are subject to recall by the voters of the State or political subdivision from which elected. Procedures and grounds for recall shall be prescribed by the legislature.

ARTICLE XII
GENERAL PROVISIONS

State Boundaries

SECTION 1. The State of Alaska shall consist of all the territory, together with the territorial waters appurtenant thereto, included in the Territory of Alaska upon the date of ratification of this constitution by the people of Alaska.

Inter-governmental Relations

SECTION 2. The State and its political subdivisions may cooperate with the United States and its territories, and with other states and their political subdivisions on matters of common interest. The respective legislative bodies may make appropriations for this purpose.

Office of Profit

SECTION 3. Service in the armed forces of the United States or the State is not an office or position of profit as the term is used in this constitution.

Disqualification for Disloyalty

SECTION 4. No person who advocates, or who aids or belongs to any party or organization or association which advocates, the overthrow by force or violence of the government of the United States or of the State shall be qualified to hold any public office of trust or profit under this constitution.

Oath of Office

SECTION 5. All public officers, before entering upon the duties of their offices, shall take and subscribe to the following oath or affirmation: "I do solemnly swear (or affirm) that I will support and defend the Constitution of the United States and the Constitution of the State of Alaska, and that I will faithfully discharge my duties as _____ to the best of my ability." The legislature may prescribe further oaths or affirmations.

Merit System

SECTION 6. The legislature shall establish a system under which the merit principle will govern the employment of persons by the State.

Retirement Systems

SECTION 7. Membership in employee retirement systems of the State or its political subdivisions shall constitute a contractual relationship. Accrued benefits of these systems shall not be diminished or impaired.

Residual Power

SECTION 8. The enumeration of specified powers in this constitution shall not be construed as limiting the powers of the State.

Provisions Self-executing

SECTION 9. The provisions of this constitution shall be construed to be self-executing whenever possible.

Interpretation

SECTION 10. Titles and subtitles shall not be used in construing this constitution. Personal pronouns used in this constitution shall be construed as including either sex.

Law-making Power

SECTION 11. As used in this constitution, the terms "by law" and "by the legislature," or variations of these terms, are used interchangeably when related to law-making powers. Unless clearly inapplicable, the law-making powers assigned to the legislature may be exercised by the people through the initiative, subject to the limitations of Article XI.

Disclaimer and Agreement

SECTION 12. The State of Alaska and its people forever disclaim all right and title in or to any property belonging to the United States or subject to its disposition, and not granted or confirmed to the State or its political subdivisions, by or under the act admitting Alaska to the Union. The State and its people further disclaim all right or title in or to any property, including fishing rights, the right or title to which may be held by or for any Indian, Eskimo, or Aleut, or community thereof, as that right or title is defined in the act of admission. The State and its people agree that, unless otherwise provided by Congress, the property, as described in this section, shall remain subject to the absolute disposition of the United States. They further agree that no taxes will be imposed upon any such property, until otherwise provided by the Congress. This tax exemption shall not apply to property held by individuals in fee without restrictions on alienation.

Consent to Act of Admission

SECTION 13. All provisions of the act admitting Alaska to the Union which reserve rights or powers to the United States, as well as those prescribing the terms or conditions of the grants of lands or other property, are consented to fully by the State and its people.

ARTICLE XIII
AMENDMENT AND REVISION

Amendments

SECTION 1. Amendments to this constitution may be proposed by a two-thirds vote of each house of the legislature. The lieutenant governor shall prepare a ballot title and proposition summarizing each proposed amendment, and shall place them on the ballot for the next general election. If a majority of the votes cast on the proposition favor the amendment, it shall be adopted. Unless otherwise provided in the amendment, it becomes effective thirty days after the certification of the election returns by the lieutenant governor.

(An amendment to this section, approved by the voters August 27, 1974, and effective October 12, 1974, changed "statewide" to read "general" in the second sentence.)

Convention

SECTION 2. The legislature may call constitutional conventions at any time.

Call by Referendum

SECTION 3. If, during any ten-year period a constitutional convention has not been held, the lieutenant governor shall place on the ballot for the next general election the question: "Shall there be a Constitutional Convention?" If a majority of the votes cast on the question are in the negative, the question need not be placed on the ballot until the end of the next ten-year period. If a a majority of the votes cast on the question are in the negative, the question need not be placed on the ballot until the end of the next ten-year period. If a majority of the votes cast on the question are in the affirmative, delegates to the convention shall be chosen at the next regular statewide election, unless the legislature provides for the election of the delegates at a special election. The lieutenant governor shall issue the call for the convention. Unless other provisions have been made by law, the call shall conform as nearly as possible to the act calling the Alaska Constitutional Convention of 1955, including, but not limited to, number of members, districts, election and certification of delegates, and submission and ratification of revisions and ordinances. The appropriation provisions of the call shall be self-executing and shall constitute a first claim on the state treasury.

Powers

SECTION 4. Constitutional conventions shall have plenary power to amend or revise the constitution, subject only to ratification by the people. No call for a constitutional convention shall limit these powers of the convention.

ARTICLE XIV
APPORTIONMENT SCHEDULE

Election Districts

SECTION 1. [This is not the original text of Section 1 but the text reflecting the latest reapportionment order.] Members of the house of representatives shall, according to the reapportionment proclamation of the governor, dated February 15, 1984, be elected from the election districts and in the numbers shown on next page.

Election District	Name of District	Number of Representatives	
1	Ketchikan-Wrangell-Petersburg	2	(Seats A & B)
2	Inside Passage	1	
3	Baranof-Chichagof	1	
4	Juneau	2	(Seats A & B)
5	Kenai-Cook Inlet	2	(Seats A & B)
6	Prince William Sound	1	
7	North Kenai-South Anchorage	1	
8	Campbell-Hillside	2	(Seats A & B)
9	Turnagain-Sand Lake	2	(Seats A & B)
10	Midtown	2	(Seats A & B)
11	Spenard	2	(Seats A & B)
12	Downtown	2	(Seats A & B)
13	Elmendorf AFB-Mountain View	2	(Seats A & B)
14	South Muldoon	2	(Seats A & B)
15	Chugiak-Eagle River-Fort Richardson	2	(Seats A & B)
16	Matanuska-Susitna	2	(Seats A & B)
17	Interior Highways	1	
18	Southeast North Star Borough	1	
19	Outer Fairbanks	1	
20	Fairbanks City	2	(Seats A & B)
21	West Fairbanks	1	
22	North Slope-Kotzebue	1	
23	Norton Sound	1	
24	Interior Rivers	1	
25	Lower Kuskokwim	1	
26	Bristol Bay-Aleutian Islands	1	
27	Kodiak-East Alaska Peninsula	1	

Senate Districts

SECTION 2. [This is not the original text of Section 2 but the text reflecting the latest reapportionment order.] Members of the senate shall, according to the reapportionment proclamation of the governor, dated February 15, 1984, be elected from the election districts and in the numbers shown below:

Senate District	Composed of Election Districts	Number of Senators	
A	Ketchikan-Wrangell-Petersburg	1	
B	Inside Passage-Baranof-Chichagof	1	
C	Juneau	1	
D	Kenai-Cook Inlet	1	
E	Prince William Sound-North Kenai-South Anchorage-Matanuska-Susitna	2	(Seats A & B)
F	Campbell-Hillside-Midtown	2	(Seats A & B)
G	Turnagain-Sand Lake-Spenard	2	(Seats A & B)
H	Downtown-Elmendorf AFB-Mountain View	2	(Seats A & B)

Senate District	Composed of Election Districts	Number of Senators
I	Muldoon-Chugiak-Eagle River-Fort Richardson	2 (Seats A & B)
J	Interior Highways-Southeast North Star Borough	1
K	Outer Fairbanks-Fairbanks City-West Fairbanks	2 (Seats A & B)
L	North Slope-Kotzebue-Norton Sound	1
M	Interior River-Lower Kuskokwim	1
N	Bristol Bay-Aleutian Islands-Kodiak-East Alaska Peninsula	1

Description of Election Districts

SECTION 3. The election districts set out in Section 1 include the following territory, in accordance with the proclamation of the governor, dated February 15, 1984:

1. **Ketchikan-Wrangell-Petersburg**—District 1 is an area within a line proceeding from Dixon Entrance in a northerly direction up Clarence Strait, passing west of Zarembo Island, northerly up Duncan Canal, across Frederick Sound to a point west of Cape Fanshaw, then northeasterly to the Canadian border and southerly along the Canadian border to the point of beginning at Dixon Entrance, excluding the area on Annette Island. The district includes the Ketchikan Gateway Borough, Wrangell, Petersburg, Hyder, Saxman, Meyers Chuck, and Kupreanof. It has a population of 16,601.58 and a variance of -9.9 percent. It will elect two house members to designated seats and one senator.

2. **Inside Passage**—District 2 is composed of that portion of Southeast Alaska between Dixon Entrance and Boundary Point 187 on the U.S./Canadian International Boundary that is not contained in Districts 1, 3, and 4. Included within its boundaries are the communities of Yakutat, Haines, Skagway, Klukwan, Gustavus, Hoonah, Angoon, Kake, Metlakatla, Thorne Bay, Klawock, Craig, and Hydaburg. The district has a population of 8,924.35 and a variance of -3.1 percent. It will elect one house member and, with District 3, one senator.

3. **Baranof-Chichagof**—District 3 consists of Baranof Island, Yakobi Island, Chichagof Island, and all of the smaller adjacent islands offshore, excluding the area within the City of Hoonah. The communities on the islands include Sitka, Pelican, Elfin Cove, Tenakee Springs, and Port Alexander. The district has a population of 8,448.97 and a variance of -8.3 percent. It will elect one house member and, with District 2, one senator.

4. **Juneau**—District 4 boundaries coincide with those of the City and Borough of Juneau. The district has a population of 19,332.75 and a variance of +4.9 percent. It will elect two house members to designated seats and one senator.

5. Kenai-Cook Inlet—District 5 includes all of the coastal areas on the east and west sides of Cook Inlet inside the Kenai Peninsula Borough, that lie south and west of Nikiski. Communities within the district include Kenai, Soldotna, Sterling, Ninilchik, Anchor Point, Homer, Seldovia, Port Graham, and English Bay. The district has a population of 19,189.95 and a variance of +4.2 percent. It will elect two house members to designated seats and one senator.

6. Prince William Sound—District 6 includes the area along Prince William Sound from Boundary Point 187 on the U.S./Canadian International Boundary on the east to the Kenai National Moose Range boundary on the west. Included in the district are the communities of Hope, Cooper Landing, Moose Pass, Seward, Whittier, Valdez, Chitina, McCarthy, Tatitlek, and Cordova. It has a population of 8,753.19 and a variance of -4.9 percent. It will elect one house member and, with Districts 7 and 16, two senators to designated seats.

7. North Kenai-South Anchorage—District 7 contains the Nikiski area on the northern Kenai Peninsula, and the southeastern reaches of the Municipality of Anchorage, including the community council areas of Old Seward/Oceanview, Rabbit Creek, Turnagain Arm, and Girdwood Valley. Its northern boundary proceeds east from Turnagain Arm along Klatt Road to the New Seward Highway, southerly on the New Seward Highway to Huffman Road, westerly along Huffman Road to the Old Seward Highway, southerly on the Old Seward Highway to DeArmoun Road, east on DeArmoun Road to Rabbit Creek, and easterly and southerly along Rabbit Creek. The district has a population of 9,580.1 and a variance of +4.0 percent. It will elect one house member and, with Districts 6 and 16, two senators to designated seats.

8. Campbell-Hillside—District 8 is bounded on the south by Rabbit Creek, DeArmoun Road, the Seward Highway, and Klatt Road, and on the west by Turnagain Arm. Dimond Boulevard and Abbott Road form the northern boundary, and the Chugach Mountains are the eastern boundary. This district includes the neighborhood council areas of Bayshore/Klatt, Huffman/O'Malley, Mid-Hillside, Hillside East and Glen Alps. The district has a population of 19,230.7 and a variance of +4.4 percent. It will elect two house members to designated seats and, with District 10, two senators to designated seats.

9. Turnagain-Sand Lake—District 9 is bounded by a line beginning at Turnagain Arm and proceeding east on Dimond Boulevard to Arctic Boulevard, then north to International Airport Road, then west to Spenard Road, then northerly to Fish Creek and continuing north to W. 36th Avenue, then west to Wisconsin Street and north on Wisconsin to Northern Lights Boulevard, then east on Northern Lights to Minnesota Drive and north on Minnesota Drive to Chester Creek, then west on Chester Creek to Knik Arm. The district includes the community council areas of Turnagain and Sand Lake. It has a population of 19,155.9 and a variance of +4.0 percent. It will elect two house members to designated seats and, with District 11, two senators to designated seats.

10. Midtown—District 10 is bounded by a line beginning at the intersection of Arctic Boulevard and Dimond Boulevard, then north to International Airport Road, east to the Old Seward Highway, north to Chester Creek, easterly to Bragaw Street and E. 20th Avenue, east to Pine Street, south to Tudor Road, then westerly and southerly along the Bureau of Land Management boundary to Birch Road, south to Abbott Road, and west along Abbott Road to the New Seward Highway, north to Dimond Boulevard, and west to the point of beginning. The district includes the community council areas of Rogers Park, Tudor, Taku-Campbell, Lake Otis, and University. It has a population of 18,183.5 and a variance of -1.3 percent. It will elect two house members to designated seats and, with District 8, two senators to designated seats.

11. Spenard—District 11 is bounded by District 10 on the east, International Airport Road on the south, Wisconsin Street, Fish Creek, and Spenard Road on the west, and Chester Creek and W. 23rd Avenue on the north. It includes the community council areas of Spenard and North Star. It has a population of 18,804.1 and a variance of +2.1 percent. It will elect two house members to designated seats and, with District 9, two senators to designated seats.

12. Downtown—District 12 is bounded by Chester Creek on the south, Bragaw Road on the east, Commercial Drive and the Elmendorf reservation boundary on the north and the inlet on the west. Included are the community council areas of Government Hill, Downtown, Penland Park, South Addition, Fairview, and parts of the areas of North Mountain View and Airport Heights. The district has a population of 18,678.4 and a variance of +1.4 percent. It will elect two house members to designated seats and, with District 13, two senators to designated seats.

13. Elmendorf Air Force Base-Mountain View—District 13 is bounded by a line beginning at the intersection of Bragaw Street and E. 20th Avenue proceeding east to Baxter Road, north to DeBarr Avenue, east to Muldoon Road, north to E. 4th Avenue, west to Patterson Street, north to the Glenn Highway, east on the Glenn Highway to the common boundary between Elmendorf Air Force Base and Fort Richardson, then following the Elmendorf military reservation boundary to Commercial Drive, then east to Mountain View Drive, then southwesterly to the Glenn Highway, then east to Bragaw Road and south to the point of beginning. The district includes the community council areas of Russian Jack Park, North and South Mountain View, Airport Heights, and North Muldoon. It has a population of 19,173.1 and a variance of +4.1 percent. It will elect two house members to designated seats and, with District 12, two senators to designated seats.

14. South Muldoon—District 14 includes Stuckagain Heights and the community council areas of Northeast, South Muldoon, and Scenic Park. The district is bounded by District 13 on the north, District 15 on the north and east, District 8 on the east and south, and District 10 on the south and west. District 14 has a population of 18,265.4 and a variance of -.8 percent. It will elect two house members to designated seats and, with District 15, two senators to designated seats.

15. Chugiak-Eagle River-Fort Richardson—District 15 includes the northern portion of the Municipality of Anchorage from Fort Richardson on the west to the municipality's border on the north and east, and by District 14 on the south. It includes the community council areas of Eklutna Valley, Chugiak, Birchwood, and Eagle River Valley. Also included are Fort Richardson, and the area of the North Muldoon Community Council area bounded by Chester Creek, Muldoon Road, E. 4th Avenue, Patterson Street, and the Glenn Highway. The district has a population of 18,395 and a variance of -.1 percent. It will elect two house members to designated seats and, with District 14, two senators to designated seats.

16. Matanuska-Susitna—District 16 is comprised of the Matanuska-Susitna Borough, including the communities of Talkeetna, Willow, Houston, Big Lake, Wasilla, Bodenburg Butte, Palmer, Sutton, Peters Creek, Montana, and Chickaloon. It has a population of 17,692.23 and a variance of -3.9 percent. It will elect two house members to designated seats and, with Districts 6 and 7, two senators to designated seats.

17. Interior Highways—District 17 is made up of those areas outside of the Matanuska-Susitna Borough and the Fairbanks North Star Borough which are along the Glenn, Parks, Richardson, and Alaska Highways. Included are Paxson, Gulkana, Glennallen, Copper Center, Tonsina, Tazlina, Eagle, Delta, Fort Greely, Tanacross, Tok, Tetlin, Northway, Nenana, Anderson, Healy, and Cantwell. The district has a population of 8,753.57 and a variance of -4.9 percent. It will elect one house member and, with District 18, one senator.

18. Southeast North Star Borough—District 18 encompasses the southeast section of the Fairbanks North Star Borough. It includes North Pole, Eielson Air Force Base, Salcha, and Harding Lake. Its population is 9,300, with a variance of +.9 percent. It will elect one house member and, with District 17, one senator.

19. Outer Fairbanks—District 19 includes Livengood, Ester, Goldstream Road, the Steese Highway, the eastern half of Farmers Loop Road, Fort Wainwright, Chena Hot Springs Road, Circle, Central, and Circle Hot springs. It has a population of 8,934.3 and a variance of -3.0 percent. It will elect one house member and, with Districts 20 and 21, two senators to designated seats.

20. Fairbanks City—District 20 is bounded by the Noyes Slough and University Avenue on the west, the Fairbanks International Airport on the southwest, the Tanana River on the south, and Fort Wainwright on the east. The Creamers Field area is included as the northern edge of the district. The district has a population of 18,319.7 and a variance of -.5 percent. It will elect two house members to designated seats and, with Districts 19 and 21, two senators to designated seats.

21. West Fairbanks—District 21 includes the western half of Farmers Loop Road and the area west of Noyes slough and University Avenue to, but not including, the Ester area. It has a population of 9,247.1 and a variance of +.4 percent. It will elect one house member and, with Districts 19 and 20, two senators to designated seats.

22. North Slope-Kotzebue—District 22 includes the areas of the North Slope Borough, Arctic Slope Regional Corporation, and the Northwest Alaska Native Association. It has a population of 8,999.06 and a variance of -2.3 percent. The district will elect one house member and, with District 23, one senator.

23. Norton Sound—District 23 includes the area of the Bering Straits Regional Corporation, Shishmaref, Diomede, Teller, Nome, Koyuk and Saint Michael, and the coastal communities as far south as Hooper Bay and Paimiut. Chevak is also included along with Yukon River villages downriver from Mountain Village. The district has a population of 9,338.86 and a variance of +1.4 percent. It will elect one house member and, with District 22, one senator.

24. Interior Rivers—District 24 includes the communities on or near the great interior rivers, the Yukon, the Koyukuk, and the Kuskokwim, as far downriver as Mountain Village on the Yukon and Tuluksak on the Kuskokwim. The district has a population of 8,936.12 and a variance of -3.0 percent. It will elect one house member and, with District 25, one senator.

25. Lower Kuskokwim—District 25 includes the Kuskokwim River communities downriver from Akiak and Akiachak, and the coastal communities from Newtok to Platinum. It has a population of 9,432.35 and a variance of +2.4 percent. It will elect one house member and, with District 24, one senator.

26. Bristol Bay-Aleutian Islands—District 26 includes all of the Bristol Bay Native Corporation area except Ivanof Bay, Perryville, Chignik Lake, Chignik, and Chignik Lagoon. Included are the remainder of the Alaska Peninsula communities, the Aleutian communities, the Bristol Bay communities as far west as Twin Hills, and communities as far upriver as Aleknagik and Koliganek. The Bristol Bay Borough is also included. The district has a population of 9,157.61 and a variance of -.6 percent. It will elect one house member and, with District 27, one senator.

27. Kodiak-East Alaska Peninsula—District 27 covers the Kodiak Island Borough and the Alaska Peninsula communities of Ivanof Bay, Perryville, Chignik Lake, Chignik, and Chignik Lagoon. It has a population of 9,592.4 and a variance of +4.1 percent. It will elect one house member and, with District 26, one senator.

ARTICLE XV
SCHEDULE OF TRANSITIONAL MEASURES

To provide an orderly transition from a territorial to a state form of government, it is declared and ordained:

Continuance of Laws	SECTION 1. All laws in force in the Territory of Alaska on the effective date of this constitution and consistent therewith shall continue in force until they expire by their own limitation, are amended, or repealed.
Saving of Existing Rights and Liabilities	SECTION 2. Except as otherwise provided in this constitution, all rights, titles, actions, suits, contracts, and liabilities and all civil, criminal, or administrative proceedings shall continue unaffected by the change from territorial to state government, and the State shall be the legal successor to the Territory in these matters.
Local Government	SECTION 3. Cities, school districts, health districts, public utility districts, and other local subdivisions of government existing on the effective date of this constitution shall continue to exercise their powers and functions under existing law, pending enactment of legislation to carry out the provisions of this constitution. New local subdivisions of government shall be created only in accordance with this constitution.
Continuance of Office	SECTION 4. All officers of the Territory, or under its laws, on the effective date of this constitution shall continue to perform the duties of their offices in a manner consistent with this constitution until they are superseded by officers of the State.
Corresponding Qualifications	SECTION 5. Residence, citizenship, or other qualifications under the Territory may be used toward the fulfillment of corresponding qualifications required by this constitution.
Governor to Proclaim Election	SECTION 6. When the people of the Territory ratify this constitution and it is approved by the duly constituted authority of the United States, the governor of the Territory shall, within thirty days after receipt of the official notification of such approval, issue a proclamation and take necessary measures to hold primary and general elections for all state elective offices provided for by this constitution.
First State Elections	SECTION 7. The primary election shall take place not less than forty nor more than ninety days after the proclamation by the governor of the Territory. The general election shall take place not less than ninety days after the primary election. The elections shall be governed by this constitution and by applicable territorial laws.
United States Senators and Representatives	SECTION 8. The officers to be elected at the first general election shall include two senators and one representative to serve in the Congress of the United States, unless senators and a representative have been previously elected and seated. One senator shall be elected for the long term and one senator for the short term, each term to expire on the third day of January in an odd-numbered year to be determined by authority of the United States. The terms of the representative shall expire on the third day of January in the odd-numbered year immediately following his assuming office. If the first representative is elected in an even-numbered year to take office in that year, a representative shall be elected at the same time to fill the full term commencing on the third day of January of the following year, and the same person may be elected for both terms.

First Governor and Lieutenant Governor: Terms	SECTION 9. The first governor and lieutenant governor shall hold office for a term beginning with the day on which they assume office and ending at noon on the first Monday in December of the even-numbered year following the next presidential election. This term shall count as a full term for purposes of determining eligibility for reelection only if it is four years or more in duration.
Election of First Senators	SECTION 10. At the first state general election, one senator shall be chosen for a two-year term from each of the following senate districts, described in Section 2 of Article XIV: A, B, D, E, G, I, J, L, N, and O. At the same election, one senator shall be chosen for a four-year term from each of the following senate districts, described in Section 2 of Article XIV: A, C, E, F, H, J, K, M, N, and P.
Terms of First State Legislators	SECTION 11. The first state legislators shall hold office for a term beginning with the day on which they assume office and ending at noon on the fourth Monday in January after the next general election, except that senators elected for four-year terms shall serve an additional two years thereafter. If the first general election is held in an even-numbered year, it shall be deemed to be the general election for that year.
Election Returns	SECTION 12. The returns of the first general election shall be made, canvassed, and certified in the manner prescribed by law. The governor of the Territory shall certify the results to the President of the United States.
Assumption of Office	SECTION 13. When the President of the United States issues a proclamation announcing the results of the election, and the State has been admitted into the Union, the officers elected and qualified shall assume office.
First Session of Legislature	SECTION 14. The governor shall call a special session of the first state legislature within thirty days after the presidential proclamation unless a regular session of the legislature falls within that period. The special session shall not be limited as to duration.
First Legislators: Office Holding	SECTION 15. The provisions of Section 5 of Article II shall not prohibit any member of the first state legislature from holding any office or position created during his first term.
First Judicial Council	SECTION 16. The first members of the judicial council shall, notwithstanding Section 8 of Article IV, be appointed for terms as follows: three attorney members for one, three, and five years respectively, and three non-attorney members for two, four, and six years respectively. The six members so appointed shall, in accordance with Section 5 of Article IV, submit to the governor nominations to fill the initial vacancies on the superior court and the supreme court, including the office of chief justice. After the initial vacancies on the superior and supreme courts are filled, the chief justice shall assume his seat on the judicial council.

Transfer of Court Jurisdiction	SECTION 17. Until the courts provided for in Article IV are organized, the courts, their jurisdiction, and the judicial system shall remain as constituted on the date of admission unless otherwise provided by law. When the state courts are organized, new actions shall be commenced and filed therein, and all causes, other than those under the jurisdiction of the United States, pending in the courts existing on the date of admission, shall be transferred to the proper state court as though commenced, filed, or lodged in those courts in the first instance, except as otherwise provided by law.
Territorial Assets and Liabilities	SECTION 18. The debts and liabilities of the Territory of Alaska shall be assumed and paid by the State, and debts owed to the Territory shall be collected by the State. Assets and records of the Territory shall become the property of the State.
First Reapportionment	SECTION 19. The first reapportionment of the house of representatives shall be made immediately following the official reporting of the 1960 decennial census, or after the first regular legislative session if the session occurs thereafter, notwithstanding the provision as to time contained in Section 3 of Article VI. All other provisions of Article VI shall apply in the first reapportionment.
State Capital	SECTION 20. The capital of the State of Alaska shall be at Juneau.
Seal	SECTION 21. The seal of the Territory, substituting the word "State" for "Territory," shall be the seal of the State.
Flag	SECTION 22. The flag of the Territory shall be the flag of the State.
Special Voting Provision	SECTION 23. Citizens who legally voted in the general election of November 4, 1924, and who meet the residence requirements for voting, shall be entitled to vote notwithstanding the provisions of Section 1 of Article V.
Ordinances	SECTION 24. Ordinance No. 1 on ratification of the constitution, Ordinance No. 2 on the Alaska-Tennessee Plan, and Ordinance No. 3 on the abolition of fish traps, adopted by the Alaska Constitutional Convention and appended to this constitution, shall be submitted to the voters and if ratified shall become effective as provided in each ordinance.
Effective Date	SECTION 25. This constitution shall take effect immediately upon the admission of Alaska into the Union as a state.
Appropriations	SECTION 26. If a majority of those voting on the question at the general election in 1982 approve the ballot proposition for the total cost to the State of providing for relocation of the capital, no additional voter approval of appropriations for that purpose within the cost approved by the voters is required under the 1982 amendment limiting increases in appropriations (Article IX, Section 16).

(The addition of this section, as an amendment to Article XV, was approved by the voters of the State November 2, 1982. However, disapproval of ballot measure 8, relating to the expenditure of $2.8 billion to relocate the capital, makes the section inoperative.)

Reconsideration of Amendment Limiting Increase in Appropriations

SECTION 27. If the 1982 amendment limiting appropriation increases (Article IX, Section 16) is adopted, the lieutenant governor shall cause the ballot title and proposition for the amendment to be placed on the ballot again at the general election in 1986. If the majority of those voting on the proposition in 1986 rejects the amendment, it shall be repealed.

(The addition of this section, as an amendment to Article XV, was approved by voters November 2, 1982. Voters in the 1986 general election voted to retain the spending limitation.)

Application of Amendment

SECTION 28. The 1982 amendment limiting appropriation increases (Article IX, Section 16) applies to appropriations made for fiscal year 1984 and thereafter.

(The addition of this section, as an amendment to Article XV, was approved by voters November 2, 1982.)

Agreed upon by the delegates in Constitutional Convention assembled at the University of Alaska, this fifth day of February, in the year of our Lord one thousand nine hundred and fifty-six, and of the Independence of the United States the one hundred and eightieth.

WM. A. EGAN
President of the Convention

R. ROLLAND ARMSTRONG
DOROTHY J. AWES
FRANK BARR
JOHN C. BOSWELL
SEABORN J. BUCKALEW, JR.
JOHN B. COGHILL
E. B. COLLINS
GEORGE D. COOPER
JOHN M. CROSS
EDWARD V. DAVIS
JAMES P. DOOGAN
TRUMAN C. EMBERG
HELEN FISCHER
VICTOR FISCHER
DOUGLAS GRAY
THOMAS C. HARRIS
JOHN S. HELLENTHAL
MILDRED R. HERMANN
HERB HILSCHER
JACK HINCKEL
JAMES HURLEY
MAURICE T. JOHNSON
YULE F. KILCHER

MAYNARD D. LONDBORG
STEVE McCUTCHEON
GEORGE M. McLAUGHLIN
ROBERT J. McNEALY
JOHN A. McNEES
M. R. MARSTON
IRWIN L. METCALF
LESLIE NERLAND
JAMES NOLAN
KATHERINE D. NORDALE
FRANK PERATROVICH
CHRIS POULSEN
PETER L. READER
BURKE RILEY
RALPH J. RIVERS
VICTOR C. RIVERS
JOHN H. ROSSWOG
B. D. STEWART
W. O. SMITH
GEORGE SUNDBORG
DORA M. SWEENEY
WARREN A. TAYLOR
H. R. VANDERLEEST

LEONARD H. KING
WILLIAM W. KNIGHT
W. W. LAWS
ELDOR R. LEE

M. J. WALSH
BARRIE M. WHITE
ADA B. WIEN

ATTEST:
THOMAS B. STEWART
Secretary of the Convention

ORDINANCE NO. 1
RATIFICATION OF CONSTITUTION

Election

SECTION 1. The Constitution for the State of Alaska agreed upon by the delegates to the Alaska Constitutional Convention on February 5, 1956, shall be submitted to the voters of Alaska for ratification or rejection at the territorial primary election to be held on April 24, 1956. The election shall be conducted according to existing laws regulating primary elections so far as applicable.

Ballot

SECTION 2. Each elector who offers to vote upon this constitution shall be given a ballot by the election judges which will be separate from the ballot on which candidates in the primary election are listed. Each of the propositions offered by the Alaska Constitutional Convention shall be set forth separately, but on the same ballot form. The first proposition shall be as follows:

"Shall the Constitution for the State of Alaska prepared and agreed upon by the Alaska Constitutional Convention be adopted?" Yes_____ No_____

Canvass

SECTION 3. The returns of this election shall be made to the governor of the Territory of Alaska, and shall be canvassed in substantially the manner provided by law for territorial elections.

Acceptance and Approval

SECTION 4. If a majority of the votes cast on the proposition favor the constitution, then the constitution shall be deemed to be ratified by the people of Alaska to become effective as provided in the constitution.

Submission of Constitution

SECTION 5. Upon ratification of the constitution, the governor of the Territory shall forthwith transmit a certified copy of the constitution to the President of the United States for submission to the Congress, together with a statement of the votes cast for and against ratification.

ORDINANCE NO. 2
ALASKA-TENNESSEE PLAN

Statement of Purpose

SECTION 1. The election of senators and a representative to serve in the Congress of the United States being necessary and proper to prepare for the admission of Alaska as a state of the Union, the following sections are hereby ordained, pursuant to Chapter 46, SLA 1955:

Ballot	SECTION 2. Each elector who offers to vote upon the ratification of the constitution may, upon the same ballot, vote on a second proposition, which shall be as follows: "Shall Ordinance Number Two (Alaska-Tennessee Plan) of the Alaska Constitutional Convention, calling for the immediate election of two United States Senators and one United States Representative, be adopted?" Yes_____No_____
Approval	SECTION 3. Upon ratification of the constitution by the people of Alaska and separate approval of this ordinance by a majority of all votes cast for and against it, the remainder of this ordinance shall become effective.
Election of Senators and Representatives	SECTION 4. Two United States senators and one United States representative shall be chosen at the 1956 general election.
Terms	SECTION 5. One senator shall be chosen for the regular term expiring on January 3, 1963, and the other for an initial short term expiring on January 3, 1961, unless when they are seated the Senate prescribes other expiration dates. The representative shall be chosen for the regular term of two years expiring January 3, 1959.
Qualifications	SECTION 6. Candidates for senators and representative shall have the qualifications prescribed in the Constitution of the United States and shall be qualified voters of Alaska.
Other Office Holding	SECTION 7. Until the admission of Alaska as a state, the senators and representative may also hold or be nominated and elected to other offices of the United States or of the Territory of Alaska, provided that no person may receive compensation for more than one office.
Election Procedure	SECTION 8. Except as provided herein, the laws of the Territory governing elections to the office of Delegate to Congress shall, to the extent applicable, govern the election of the senators and representative. Territorial and other officials shall perform their duties with reference to this election accordingly.
Independent Candidates	SECTION 9. Persons not representing any political party may become independent candidates for the offices of senator or representative by filing applications in the manner provided in Section 38-5-10, ACLA 1949, insofar as applicable. Applications must be filed in the office of the director of finance of the Territory on or before June 30, 1956.
Party Nominations	SECTION 10. Party nominations for senators and representative shall, for this election only, be made by party conventions in the manner prescribed in Section 38-4-11, ACLA 1949, for filling a vacancy in a party nomination occurring after a primary election. The names of the candidates nominated shall be certified by the chairman and secretary of the central committee of each political party to the director of finance of the Territory on or before June 30, 1956.

Certification	SECTION 11. The director of finance shall certify the names of all candidates for senators and representative to the clerks of court by July 15, 1956. The clerks of court shall cause the names to be printed on the official ballot for the general election. Independent candidates shall be identified as provided in Section 38-5-10, ACLA 1949. Candidates nominated at party conventions shall be identified with appropriate party designations as is provided by law for nominations at primary elections.
Ballot Form; Who Elected	SECTION 12. The ballot form shall group separately the candidates seeking the regular senate term, those seeking the short senate term, and candidates for representative. The candidate for each office receiving the largest number of votes cast for that office shall be elected.
Duties and Emoluments	SECTION 13. The duties and emoluments of the offices of senator and representative shall be as prescribed by law.
Convention Assistance	SECTION 14. The president of the Alaska Constitutional Convention, or a person designated by him, may assist in carrying out the purposes of this ordinance. The unexpended and unobligated funds appropriated to the Alaska Constitutional Convention by Chapter 46, SLA 1955, may be used to defray expenses attributable to the referendum and the election required by this ordinance.
Alternate Effective Dates	SECTION 15. If the Congress of the United States seats the senators and representative elected pursuant to this ordinance and approves the constitution before the first election of state officers, then Section 25 of Article XV shall be void and shall be replaced by the following:

"The provisions of the constitution applicable to the first election of state officers shall take effect immediately upon the admission of Alaska into the Union as a state. The remainder of the constitution shall take effect when the elected governor takes office."

ORDINANCE NO. 3
ABOLITION OF FISH TRAPS

Ballot	SECTION 1. Each elector who offers to vote upon the ratification of the constitution may, upon the same ballot, vote on a third proposition, which shall be as follows:

"Shall Ordinance Number Three of the Alaska Constitutional Convention, prohibiting the use of fish traps for the taking of salmon for commercial purposes in the coastal waters of the State, be adopted?" Yes _____ No _____

Effect of Referendum	SECTION 2. If the constitution shall be adopted by the electors and if a majority of all the votes cast for and against this ordinance favor its adoption, then the following shall become operative upon the effective date of the constitution:

146 / Reaching for a Star

"As a matter of immediate public necessity, to relieve economic distress among individual fishermen and those dependent upon them for a livelihood, to conserve the rapidly dwindling supply of salmon in Alaska, to insure fair competition among those engaged in commercial fishing, and to make manifest the will of the people of Alaska, the use of fish traps for the taking of salmon for commercial purposes is hereby prohibited in all the coastal waters of the State."

Appendix 3
Amendments to Constitution

Year Approved By Voters	Amendment	Article, Section Affected
1966	Changed "He" to "A voter" and provided that separate residency requirements for voting in presidential elections could be prescribed by law.	V: 1
1968	Provided for creation of a Commission on Judicial Qualifications and compensation of commission members.	IV: 10, 13
1970	Lowered voting age from nineteen to eighteen.	V: 1
1970	Changed name of secretary of state to lieutenant governor.	III: 7-11
1970	Provided for selection of chief justice of supreme court by majority of court (chief justice previously appointed by governor from among persons nominated by judicial council); administrative director of court system to serve at pleasure of court (director previously served at chief justice's pleasure).	IV: 2, 16
1970	Eliminated requirement of ability to read or speak English as a prerequisite for voting.	V: 1

Year Approved By Voters	Amendment	Article, Section Affected
1972	Amended exclusive right of fishery provision.	VIII: 15
1972	Added "sex" to section.	I: 3
1972	Added section guaranteeing right to privacy.	I: 22
1972	Inserted "residency" in first sentence and deleted voting requirement of one year's residence in Alaska.	V: 1
1972	Eliminated requirement of city and noncity representation on borough assembly, opening way for borough-wide election of assembly members.	X: 4
1974	Changed "statewide election" to "general election" in second sentence.	XIII: 1
1976	Authorized legislature to reconsider vetoed bills during special sessions and prescribed other procedures for dealing with such bills.	II: 9, 16
1976	Provided for establishment of Alaska Permanent Fund.	IX: 7, 15
1982	Changed name of Commission on Judicial Qualifications to Commission on Judicial Conduct and changed composition of commission membership.	IV: 10
1982	Imposed limitation on state appropriations.	IX: 16 XV: 26, 27, 28

Year Approved By Voters	Amendment	Article, Section Affected
1982	Authorized incurrence of state indebtedness for housing loans for veterans.	IX: 8
1984	Limited length of legislative sessions.	II: 8
1988	Added resident preference section.	I: 23

Notes

Introduction

1. J. Gerald Williams, letter to Governor B. Frank Heintzleman, 28 September 1955, Legislative Affairs Agency files, Juneau, Alaska.
2. A similar provision was included in the Alaska Constitution and in 1976 forced the resignation of Commissioner of Administration Andrew Warwick. Warwick resigned from the Alaska House of Representatives on December 9, 1974, to accept appointment as commissioner, the salary for which had been increased by the legislature in which Warwick had served. Several legislators brought suit to nullify the appointment, citing the constitutional prohibition. The matter went to the Alaska Supreme Court whose ruling on January 8, 1976, removed Warwick from office for twelve days, the remainder of the one-year constitutional ban. At the end of that period, Governor Jay Hammond immediately reappointed Warwick to the position.
3. Public Law 154, approved July 12, 1955.
4. Ernest Gruening, *The State of Alaska* (New York: Random House, 1954), p. 376.
5. *Anchorage Daily Times*, 19 April 1955.
6. Victor Fischer, *Alaska's Constitutional Convention* (Fairbanks: University of Alaska Press, 1975), p. 23.

Chapter 1   *Getting Under Way*

1. The number of delegates was symbolic; there were fifty-five delegates at the federal constitutional convention in Philadelphia in 1787. Fifty-five was also considered the optimal number for the task of constitution-writing.
2. *Fairbanks Daily News-Miner*, 8 November 1955. Shortly after the convention got under way, the delegates adopted this resolution: "It is the intent of this convention that the constitution should be a document of fundamental principles of basic government, and contain only the framework for state government."
3. *News-Miner*, 12 December 1955.
4. Ernest Gruening, *Many Battles* (New York: Liveright, 1973), p. 401.
5. The convention awarded a $40,000 contract to PAS, the funds for which came from a $75,000 appropriation to the committee by the 1955 legislature.

Chapter 2 Why Statehood?

1. Hearings before a Special Subcommittee on Alaska Problems of the Committee on Merchant Marine and Fisheries, U.S. House of Representatives, 81st Congress, 1st Session, on H.R. 1515, October 24, 27, 28, 29 and November 1-9, 1949, p. 377.
2. U.S. Fish and Wildlife Service statistics, cited in *Pacific Fisherman Yearbook, 1962.*
3. George Sundborg, *Statehood for Alaska—The Issues Involved and the Facts about the Issues* (Anchorage: Alaska Statehood Association, 1946).

Chapter 3 The Fight for Statehood

1. Sundborg, *Statehood for Alaska.*
2. *Daily Alaska Empire* (Juneau), 5 February 1953.
3. See Note 2 above.
4. *Times,* 2 April 1954 (Associated Press story from Washington).
5. *Times,* 5 April 1954.
6. *Times,* 16 March 1955 (Associated Press story from Washington).
7. Hearings before the Committee on Interior and Insular Affairs, U.S. Senate, 84th Congress, 1st Session, on S. 49, S. 399, and S. 402, Washington, D.C., February 21, 22, and 28, 1955, p. 89.
8. See Note 7 above.
9. *Time* magazine, 23 May 1955.

Chapter 4 Organizing the Convention

1. Following the convention, the Alaska Statehood Committee had Gruening's address—titled "Let Us End American Colonialism"—published in pamphlet form for use in the final phase of the statehood campaign. It was distributed widely by Alaska-Tennessee Plan "Senator" Gruening to journalists, business executives, members of Congress.
2. Fischer, p. 29.
3. Conversation with Burke Riley, 17 September 1988.
4. Fischer, p. 30.
5. Fischer, p. 16.
6. *News-Miner,* 21 November 1955.
7. *News-Miner,* 14 November 1955.
8. *News-Miner,* 15 November 1955.
9. Gerald E. Bowkett, "Egan of Valdez," *Alaska Journal,* Autumn 1984, p. 28.

Chapter 5 Open or Closed Commitee Meetings?

1. *News-Miner,* 11 November 1955.
2. *News-Miner,* editorial, 14 November 1955.
3. *News-Miner,* 14 November 1955.
4. *News-Miner,* 15 November 1955 (Associated Press story from Fairbanks).
5. *News-Miner,* 21 November 1955.

Chapter 6 A One- or Two-House Legislature?

1. Fischer, p. 85.
2. By order of the governor, the Alaska Senate was reapportioned in 1965 on the basis of population, as required by the U.S. Supreme Court's landmark "one man, one vote" decision of June 15, 1964, in the case of *Reynolds v. Sims*.

Chapter 7 A New Capital?

1. *News-Miner*, 21 November 1955.
2. There was a court challenge of the section and an Alaska Supreme Court justice from the Juneau area held it was *not* a permanent provision. The 2-1 decision of the high court, handed down on August 16, 1962, was written by Associate Justice John H. Dimond, son of Anthony J. Dimond. The section could be amended by the legislature or the people through the initiative, Dimond wrote. The decision cleared the way for a vote in 1962 on capital relocation.
3. *Empire*, 23 December 1955.

Chapter 8 Appoint or Elect Judges?

1. In recognition of her "nagging wife" role, the delegates later presented her with a rolling pin autographed by each of them. *Juneau Independent*, 11 December 1955.
2. Under the constitution, the supreme court can be enlarged by law, upon its request, the superior court system solely by law. Five justices now serve on the supreme court. There are twenty-nine superior court judges, sixteen district court judges, and fifty-eight district magistrates within the state's four judicial districts. Three judges sit on the court of appeals.
3. In the 1964 general election, Harry O. Arend, an Alaska Supreme Court justice, was removed from the court by the electorate; 29,884 voted for his retention, 34,054 voted against. Arend had been caught in the cross fire of a bitter supremacy struggle between the Alaska bar and Buell A. Nesbett, chief justice of the supreme court. Nesbett did not face a retention vote in 1964. Arend did and the bar campaigned vigorously against him. Two district court judges serving in Anchorage, Joseph J. Brewer and Virgil D. Vochoska, were removed from the bench by voters in 1982.
4. Convention consultants felt the people's control of the judicial branch was diminished by exempting attorney members of the judicial council from legislative confirmation. Late in the convention they recommended the attorney members be subject to confirmation and that a superior court judge and another layman be added to the judicial council. With the convention near an end, the recommendations were not acted on. See Fischer, p. 116.

Chapter 10 Home for Christmas

1. *News-Miner*, 2 December 1955.
2. *News-Miner*, 13 December 1955.
3. *News-Miner*, 5 January 1956 (Associated Press story from Washington).
4. *News-Miner*, 6 January 1956 (Associated Press story from Washington).
5. See Note 4 above.

Chapter 14 Local Government

1. The North Slope Borough, by far the largest organized borough, spreads over approximately 88,281 square miles; the smallest, the Bristol Bay Borough, 873 square miles. The Fairbanks North Star Borough comprises 7,500 square miles, the Matanuska-Susitna Borough 20,544, the Municipality of Anchorage 1,884, the Kenai Peninsula Borough 14,697.

Chapter 15   The Legislature

1. From 1959 through the 1983 legislative session, 134 bills were vetoed in their entirety. Forty-six of these were reconsidered by the legislature and seventeen vetoes overridden. None of the reconsidered bills was an appropriation bill. From this it appears that vetoes are not casually or easily overridden.
2. The legislature met for 81 days in 1959, the first year of statehood; 88 days in 1964, the year of the Alaska earthquake; 95 days in 1969; 147 days in 1970; 161 days in 1972; 90 days in 1973; 161 days in 1978; 168 days in 1981; 152 days in 1984, the year voters approved a constitutional amendment limiting regular legislative sessions to 120 days.
3. Payment of per diem allowances to legislators is generally considered to have dulled the incentive to conclude legislative business expeditiously.
4. All members of the Alaska congressional delegation but Bob Bartlett, Ernest Gruening, and Frank Murkowski served previously in the Alaska legislature. They are Representatives Ralph J. Rivers, Howard Pollock, Nick Begich and Don Young and Senators Mike Gravel and Ted Stevens. Before statehood, Bartlett and Gruening, who were to become the state's first two senators, had served for many years as delegate to Congress and territorial governor, respectively. Senator Murkowski was state commissioner of economic development from 1966-70, in the Hickel/Miller administration.

Chapter 17   A Strong Executive

1. *News-Miner*, 5 December 1955.
2. Only one such board has been created since statehood. The Republican-controlled legislature in 1967 put a board over the Department of Education in place of a gubernatorial appointee. The board, with the approval of Governor Walter J. Hickel, selected Clifford Hartman to head the department.
3. William A. Egan voted against the amendment, undoubtedly with some misgivings. On the eve of the convention he told the *News-Miner* he favored a strong executive branch of government with a minimum of elected officials but he did feel that one office, that of attorney general, should remain elective as "a safeguard against a strong chief executive usurping the powers of his office." At a convention reunion in 1977 he urged that the office of attorney general be made elective.
4. This power was exercised massively for the first time in 1972 when Governor Egan in an economy move struck items totaling $11.3 million from the 1972-73 budget approved by the legislature.

Chapter 18   Moving against the Traps

1. *Hearings before a Special Subcommittee on Alaska Problems of the Committee on Merchant Marine and Fisheries*, pp. 284-85.

Chapter 19   Pushing for Statehood

1. *News-Miner*, 24 January 1956.
2. Naske, p. 141.
3. Fischer, p. 153.
4. *News-Miner*, 30 January 1956.

Chapter 21   The Final Days

1. *News-Miner*, 20 January 1956 (Associated Press story from Washington).
2. *News-Miner*, 25 January 1956.
3. *News-Miner*, 26 January 1956.
4. R. E. Robertson, letter to William Egan, Legislative Affairs Agency files, Juneau.
5. *Empire*, 6 February 1956.
6. William Egan, letter to R.E. Robertson, Legislative Affairs Agency files, Juneau.
7. Conversation with Burke Riley, 17 September 1988.
8. State Senator George Hohman, who had served in the legislature for sixteen years, was expelled from the upper chamber on a fifteen-to-four vote on March 2, 1982, for his conviction late in 1981 on bribery charges. This is the only such case since statehood.

Chapter 22   A Constitution for Alaska

1. *News-Miner*, 6 February 1956.
2. See Note 1 above.
3. Working under chief clerk Katherine Alexander's supervision were Bernice Black, Louise Gooch, Charlotte Taylor, Willou Bichel, Ben Potter, Betty Jean Miles, David Brown, Carolyn Oakley, Mary Diede, Irene Russell, Delores Goad and Charlie Wilson.
4. See Note 1 above.
5. See Note 1 above.
6. See Note 1 above.

Chapter 23   Winning the Fight

1. *The New York Times*, 12 February 1956.
2. Report of the Ratification Committee, 9 February 1956.
3. *News-Miner*, 6 February 1956.
4. Fischer, p. 176.
5. Commented *The New York Times* on April 30, 1956:

   "Alaska voters, by a margin of more than two to one, have now ratified the constitution that was recently drafted...

   "Certainly the citizens of Alaska have done their full share in making the case for early action on their plea for statehood. . . . It cannot be said, now, that there is not overwhelming Alaskan support for the statehood move.

   "Whether this will have any effect on Congress at this time is highly problematical. The whole campaign for statehood...bogged down some time ago because of partisan political considerations that were unworthy of an American Congress. The Alaskan vote may serve to refresh interest in the issue. . . .

   "We firmly believe that the vast majority of Americans wish to have...[Alaska and Hawaii] admitted. Both have shown themselves to be eminently qualified and our Union will be enriched by their full membership. . . ."

   Life magazine editorialized on May 14, 1956:

   "...As Hawaii did in 1950, Alaska has now held a constitutional convention...[the constitution] was approved a few days ago by a big popular majority, in the same referendum that adopted the Tennessee Plan. . . . The next step the Alaskans will take is to elect...pseudo senators and a representative. . . .

"We hope they get results...It is always a pleasure to see people claim their right to self-government, especially when it adds to the power and prestige of the U.S. Admitting Alaska and Hawaii...will certainly do that. . . ."

6. *Congressional Record*, 14 January 1957, pp. 466-69.
7. Naske, *An Interpretive History*, pp. 154-55.
8. United Press story, Washington, 26 July 1957, author's files.
9. *Washington Calling*, Senator Neuberger's weekly newsletter to constituents, 14 July 1958.
10. *Anchorage Daily Times*, 3 January 1959 (Associated Press, A. Robert Smith stories from Washington).
11. *Anchorage Daily Times*, 3 January 1959 (Associated Press stories from Juneau); *The New York Times*, 3 January 1959; conversations with several who were present at the swearing-in, including Dick Peter and Hugh J. Wade.

Suggested Reading

Alaska Legislative Council. *Minutes of the Daily Proceedings, Alaska Constitutional Convention, Parts 1-6* and *Alaska Constitutional Convention Journal, Vols. 1-2.* Juneau: Alaska Legislative Council, 1965.

Arnold, Robert D., ed. *Alaska Native Land Claims.* Anchorage: The Alaska Native Foundation, 1976, 1978.

Fischer, Victor. *Alaska's Constitutional Convention.* Fairbanks: University of Alaska Press, 1975.

Fischer, Victor and Thomas A. Morehouse. *Borough Government in Alaska.* College, Alaska: Institute of Social, Economic and Government Research, University of Alaska, 1971.

Gruening, Ernest. *Many Battles.* New York: Liveright, 1973.

Gruening, Ernest. *The State of Alaska.* New York: Random House, 1954, revised 1968.

Gruening, Ernest. *The Battle for Alaska Statehood.* College, Alaska: The University of Alaska Press in cooperation with the Alaska Purchase Centennial Commission, 1967.

Harrison, Gordon S. *Alaska's Constitution: A Citizen's Guide.* College, Alaska: Institute of Social and Economic Research, University of Alaska, 1986.

Hunt, William R. *Alaska: A Bicentennial History.* New York: W. W. Norton & Company, Inc., American Association for State and Local History, 1976.

Suggested Reading / 157

Naske, Claus-M., John S. Whitehead, and William Schneider. *Alaska Statehood: The Memory of the Battle and the Evaluation of the Present by Those Who Lived It.* Fairbanks: Alaska Statehood Commission, 1981.

Naske, Claus-M. and Herman E. Slotnick. *Alaska: A History of the 49th State.* Second edition. Norman: University of Oklahoma Press, 1987.

Naske, Claus-M. *An Interpretive History of Alaskan Statehood.* Anchorage: Alaska Northwest Publishing Company, 1973. (Revised as *A History of Alaska Statehood.* Lanham, Maryland: University Press of America, 1985.)

Naske, Claus-M. *Bob Bartlett of Alaska: A Life in Politics.* Fairbanks: University of Alaska Press, 1979.

Index

Advisory Committee on Committees, 30
Ahmoogak, Roy, 6
Alaska Air National Guard, 102
Alaska Native Claims Settlement Act, 59
Alaska Public Offices Commission, 102
Alaska Range, 22
"Alaska's Flag," 8, 90
Alaska Sportsmen's Council, 52
Alaska Statehood Association, 4
Alaska Statehood Commission, 102
Alaska Statehood Committee, 2, 6, 7, 20, 22, 91, 93, 96
Alaska Statehood Day, 103
Alaska-Tennessee Plan, 81, 83, 84, 91, 95, 96, 103
   election of delegates, 95
   Senate welcomes delegation, 95
Alexander, Katherine, 22, 92, 102
Anchorage, 2, 3, 9, 21, 25, 32, 34, 37, 46, 62, 63, 68, 86, 94, 97, 98
Anchorage Daily Times, 2, 3, 9, 79, 94
Anchorage Sportsmen's Association, 52
Anderson, Clarence, 54
An Interpretive History of Alaskan Statehood, 78
Armstrong, R. Rolland, 31, 76, 90, 102, 105
Arnold, W. C., 12
Associated Press, 5, 27, 98, 99
Atkinson, Joseph, 23
Atwood, Evangeline, 15
Atwood, Robert, 3, 7-9, 15, 16, 20, 94, 95, 99, 104
Austin E. Lathrop High School, 23
Awes (Haaland), Dorothy, 66, 102, 105

Baker, W. L., 16
Barr, Frank, 5, 31, 44, 60, 63-65, 71, 72, 105

Bartlett, Doris Ann, 22
Bartlett, E. L. (Bob), 3, 5, 6, 7, 14, 16, 17, 22, 53, 55, 79, 88, 96, 98, 99, 101, 104
Bellingham, 74
Benson, Benny, 89
Benson, Henry A., 99
Board of Fisheries and Game, 55
Boileau, George S. J., 8
Boochever, Robert, 37
Boswell, John C., 44, 65, 75, 76, 105
Boyko, Edgar Paul, 94
Bristol Bay, 76
Bristol Bay Fish Producers' Association, 76
Buckalew, Seaborn J., 32, 36, 42, 66, 75, 86, 102, 105
Burdick, Charles G., 95
Butrovich, John, 95, 98

California, 42, 76, 78, 103
Canned Salmon Industry, 3, 11, 12
Capital, Alaska State
   location debate, 34-37
Chena River, 97
Coghill, John B., 39, 54, 71, 83, 84, 102, 105
Collins, E. B., 1, 21, 23, 31, 49, 87, 92, 105
Colonialism, 21
Columbia University, 16
Commission on Judicial Conduct, 41
Commission on Judicial Qualifications, 41
Commission on the Status of Women, 102
Committee on Executive Branch, 70
Committee on Direct Legislation, Amendment and Revision, 50
Committee on Judiciary Branch, 38
Committee on Legislative Branch, 30, 64
Committee on Local Government, 60

Index / 159

Committee on Ordinances and Transitional Measures, 35, 75, 80, 82
Committee on Resolutions and Recommendations, 35
Committee on Resources, 53
Committee on Suffrage, Elections and Apportionment, 42
Constitution, 107-149
   Amendments to Constitution, 147-49
   Article I, Declaration of Rights, 108-110
   Article II, Legislature, 110-13
      salaries, gubernatorial, 111
      session, length, 111
      sessions, annual, 111
      vetoes, gubernatorial, 112-13
   Article III, Executive, 113-16
      boards and commissions, 116
      governor, 113-14
      lieutenant governor, 114-15
   Article IV, Judiciary, 116-19
      chief justice, 117
      judicial council, 117-18
      superior court, 117
      supreme court, 116-17
   Article V, Suffrage and Elections, 119-20
      voter qualifications, 119
   Arcticle VI, Legislature Apportionment, 120-21
   Article VII, Health, Education, and Welfare, 121-22
   Article VIII, Natural Resources, 122-24
   Article IX, Finance and Taxation, 124-27
   Article X, Local Government, 127-28
   Article XI, Initiative, Referendum, and Recall, 128-29
   Article XII, General Provisions, 130-31
   Article XII, Amendment and Revision, 131-32
   Article XIV, Apportionment Schedule, 132-38
      election districts, 133-38
   Article XV, Schedule of Transitional Measures, 138-42
   Ordinance No. 1, Ratification of Constitution, 143
   Ordinance No. 2, Alaska-Tennessee Plan, 143-45
   Ordinance No. 3, Abolition of Fish Traps, 145-46
Constitution Hall, 8, 47, 48, 85, 88, 90, 104
Constitutional Convention, 21, 92
   adoption by delegates, 89-90
   attorney general, 71-72

bicameral-unicameral debate, 30-33, 64, 86
boards and commissions, 70
chief clerk, 92
closing ceremony, 85, 88-92
committee meetings, 25-28
cost of, 22, 90
Davis amendment, 68-69
Declaration of Rights, 86
delegates
   candidacies, legal challenge of, 2
   election of, 2
   hometowns, 105-6
   militancy, 82-84
   occupations, 105-6
   public service, 1-2, 101-4
   restraints on, 3
   social activities, 85
   survivors, 105-6
distribution of copies of, 91, 93
election of permanent officers, 21-22
enabling act, 22
final proofreading of, 87
fish and game management, 52-56
   limited-entry program, 55-56
   placed in executive branch, 55
   no exclusive right of fishery, 55
governor, 70, 72-73
hailed nationally by experts, press, 93
hearings, 26-27
judges, appoint or elect, 38-41
legislative apportionment, 68-69, 86
legislature, 64-67
lieutenant governor, 70-71, 73
local government, 60-63
   assemblies, 61
   boroughs, 60-63
   cities, 60-61
   public utility districts, 60
   school board taxing powers, 62
   school districts, 60, 62
   representation, 61
   unification, 63
opening ceremony, 5-8
organizing, 20-24
prayers, 6, 8, 29
president, 6
president honored, 91
procedures, initiative and referendum, 49-51
ratification by voters, 95
ratification campaign, 91, 94
reapportionment, 68-69
recess, 46
reimbursement of delegates, 22

resolutions, 90-91
salaries, gubernatorial, 65-66
secretary, 6
secretary of state, 70-71, 73
session, length, 66-67
sessions, annual, 66
sessions, night, 30, 48
stimulates new interest in statehood, 93
unity, nonpartisanship, 4
vetoes, gubernatorial, 64-67
voting qualifications, 42-45
Cook Inlet, 76
Cooper, George D., 31, 40, 105
Cordova, 21
Council, Mary Lee, 99
Cross, John M., 32, 105

Daily Alaska Empire, 2
Davies, Lawrence E., 5
Davis amendment, 68, 69
Davis, Edward V., 22, 30, 32, 39, 50, 58, 61-63, 68, 69, 86, 102, 105
Dean, William F., 78
Dillingham, 76
Dimond, Anthony J., 13-16, 40, 92, 104
Doogan, James, 62, 72, 83, 85, 105
Douthit, Florence, 5, 86, 92, 103
Douthit, Jim, 5, 103

Egan, Dennis, 100
Egan, Neva, 97, 100, 104
Egan, William, 3, 10, 21, 22, 24, 30, 32, 36, 46, 47, 53, 55, 69, 78, 86-88, 90-92, 94, 95, 98-102, 104, 105
Eighty-fifth Congress, 96
Eisenhower, Dwight, 16-18, 47, 85, 96, 98, 99
Emberg, Truman C., 76, 105
Engle, Clair, 47

Fairbanks, 1, 5, 6, 8, 37, 44, 46, 62, 63, 68, 94-98
Fairbanks Daily News-Miner, 5, 24, 27, 34, 79, 86, 90-93, 96, 102
Fifty-five Club, 92
Fish and game management, 52-56
limited-entry program, 55-56
placed in executive branch, 55
no exclusive right of fishery, 55
Fish traps, 74, 77, 86
elimination, early referendum on, 12
ordinance banning traps adopted by convention, 77
White amendment, 76, 77
Fischer, Helen, 23, 105

Fishcher, Victor, 23, 25, 36, 43, 54, 61-63, 76, 102, 105
Flag, Alaska, 5, 89, 99
Florida, 95
Forbes, Vernon D., 6, 22, 94

Gabrielson, Ira N., 52
Gray, Douglas, 40, 42-44, 69, 105
Gruening, Ernest, 2, 5, 7, 14-18, 20, 22, 70, 95, 98, 99, 101, 102, 104

Hagerty, James, 100
Hall, John B. (Dixie), 6, 22
Harris, Thomas C., 32, 34, 69, 105
Hawaii, 8, 16, 17, 19, 47, 78, 96, 97, 103
Heintzleman, Frank B., 5, 6, 17, 18, 70, 89, 99
Heintzleman partition plan, 17
Hellenthal, John S., 25, 27, 39, 40, 43, 57, 68, 82, 83, 105
Hendrickson, Waino, 99
Hermann, Mildred, 1, 2, 6, 8, 16, 21, 22, 26, 29, 35, 38, 40, 47, 53, 54, 66, 92, 105
Hickel, Walter J., 17, 78, 96, 101, 102
Hilscher, Herb, 63, 66, 72, 105
Hinckel, Jack, 32, 63, 69, 105
Holland, Spessard L., 95
Homer, 29
House Committee on Interior and Insular Affairs, 19
Hurley, James, 35, 36, 50, 51, 61, 82, 91, 105
Hurley, Katherine, 22
Hutchison, James, 5

Interior Department's Division of Territories and Island Possessions, 20
Izaak Walton League, 52

Jackson, Henry, 18, 47, 97
Johnson, Maurice T., 29, 31, 42, 62, 64, 65, 105
Juneau, 3, 23, 32, 34, 36, 42, 54, 86, 87, 95, 99, 102
Juneau Independent, 26

Kederick, Robert, 2
Kennedy, John F., 99
Ketchikan, 53
Kilcher, Yule, 29, 36, 105
King, Leonard H., 105
Knight, William, 35, 77, 105
Knik Bridge, 62
Knowland, William F., 78

Kodiak, 32, 63
Kotzebue, 32

Ladd Air Force Base, 23
Ladd Air Force Base Choral Group, 88, 90
Laws, William, 105
Lee, Eldor R., 74, 84, 105
Lehleitner, George H., 78, 79, 96, 103, 104
Lockwood, George, 57, 58, 102, 103
Londborg, Maynard D., 23, 29, 34, 44, 57, 61, 64, 84, 105
Long, Russell, 95
Louisiana, 95, 103
Lyng, Howard, 2

Mandatory Borough Act, 63
Marler, Jack, 94
Marston amendment, 57, 58
Marston, M. R. (Muktuk), 43, 49, 57, 58, 82, 88, 102, 103, 106
Matanuska Valley, 35
McCarrey, Jr., J. L., 2
McCutcheon, Steve, 21, 30, 51, 54, 64, 65, 71, 83, 105
McGinnis, Fred, 47
McKay, Douglas, 19, 96
McLaughlin, George, 21, 38, 39, 42, 50, 58, 72, 80, 83, 106
McMullin, Jane, 47
McNealy, Robert J., 31, 35, 36, 38, 39, 41, 66, 75, 80, 82, 83, 102, 106
McNees, John A., 31, 32, 36, 43, 57, 66, 106
Men of the Tundra, 102
Metcalf, Irwin L., 40, 106
Miller, Alex, 78
Montana, 95
Morse, Wayne, 101
Mount McKinley, 22, 29
Murray, James E., 95

Naske, Claus-M., 78
National defense lands withdrawal, 96, 97
Native Allotment Act, 57
Natives
    convention delegate, 3
    land claims, 57-59
    Marston amendment, 57, 58
    Native Allotment Act, 57
    voting rights, 42, 43
Nebraska, 32, 96
Nerland, Leslie, 44, 82, 84, 106
Neuberger, Richard, 97
New Capital Site Planning Commission, 37
New Orleans, 78
New York, 97

New York Times, 5, 93
Nixon, Richard, 98, 99
Nolan, James, 66, 106
Nome, 2, 3, 31
Nordale Hotel, 6
Nordale, Katherine, 2, 53, 54, 80, 102, 106

Oakland Tribune, 103
O'Brien, Leo W., 97
O'Mahoney, Joseph C., 95, 96
Operation Statehood, 18, 25, 34, 87, 93, 96
Organic Act of 1912, 2, 3, 11, 35, 60, 97

Palmer, 35
Patty, Dr. Ernest N., 6, 8, 90, 91
Payne, Ancil, 87
Peratrovich, Frank, 2, 3, 5, 22, 24, 43, 66, 88, 90, 102, 106
Petersburg, 74
Phillips, Brad, 98
Portage, 62
Poulsen, Chris, 34, 106
Preston, Douglas, 6
Puget Sound, 76

Ratification Committee, 93
Rayburn, Sam, 96, 99
Reader, Peter L., 3, 106
Riley, Burke, 2, 21, 27, 32, 64, 65, 72, 73, 75, 92, 102, 106
Rivers, Ralph, 2, 3, 21-23, 25, 36, 39, 72, 83, 88, 95, 99, 101, 106
Rivers, Victor, 2, 21, 23, 32, 44, 51, 55, 62, 65, 72, 76, 81, 106
Robertson, R. E., 34-36, 43, 44, 76, 86, 87, 99, 106
Roosevelt, Pres. Franklin D., 6
Rosswog, John H., 21, 54, 60-62, 81, 106
Rules Committee, 25, 27

Salmon, resource declines, 12, 52
Salvation Army, 103
San Francisco, 74
Saturday Review, 18
Schedule of Transitional Measures, 35, 36
Seaton, Fred A., 96, 98, 99
Seattle, 74
Sheldon Jackson College, 102
Signers Hall, 5
Sitka, 35, 77, 102
Sitka Pioneers' Home, 77
Smith, W. O. (Bo), 53, 74, 76, 106
Snedden, C. W., 96
Southeastern Seine Boat Owners Association, 52

State Board of Education, 102
Statehood
    campaign movement, 14-19
    celebrations, 97
    first chief executive, 100-101
    founders of, 103
    hearings, 16
    Heintzleman partition plan, 17
    legislation, 96-97
    national interest in, 93
    prospects, 19, 79
    referendum on, 21, 98
    statehood bill, 14
    statehood bill, passage of, 97
    statehood bill, signing of, 98
    statehood proclamation, signing of, 99
    state office, candidates for, 98-99
Stepovich, Mike, 98, 99
Stevens, Ted, 94, 96, 101
Stewart, B. D., 2, 22, 35, 55, 80, 106
Stewart, Thomas B., 22, 46, 47, 102, 104
Subcommittee on Territories and Insular Affairs, 18, 47
Sundborg, George, 22, 23, 26, 39, 40, 50, 53-55, 58, 65, 66, 71, 80, 87, 92, 102, 106
Sweeney, Dora, 32, 106

Tanana Valley, 22
Tanana Valley Sportsmen's Association, 52
Taxation Without Representation, 94
Taylor, Warren A., 2, 26, 35, 36, 43, 47, 53, 54, 62, 102, 106
Tennessee Plan, 10, 78-81
    adopted by convention, 79, 81, 84
    method, 78
    nomination of congressional delegates, 79, 80

Territory of Alaska
    bureaucracy, 9-12
    limited powers of legislature, 11, 12
    population, 16
    residents denied rights, 9
The State of Alaska, 18
Time, 19
Tonkin Gulf Resolution, 101
Treaty of Cession, 14
Truman, Harry, 14, 16, 85

Unalakleet, 29, 57
United Press, 7
U.S. Fish and Wildlife Service, 52
University of Alaska, 5, 88
University of Alaska's Institute of Social, Economic and Government Research, 102

Valdez, 21, 32
Vanderleest, H. R., 35, 106
von Schneidau, Christian, 91

Wade, Hugh J., 99
Wainwright, 6
Walsh, Michael J., 2, 22, 69, 87, 106
Washington, 47
White amendment, 76, 77
White, Barrie, 34, 43, 76, 77, 81, 106
Wickersham, James, 14, 92
Wien, Ada B., 45, 91, 106
Wien, Noel, 45
Wildlife Management Institute, 52
Wilkins, Hubert, 78
Williams, J. Gerald, 2
Willow, 37
Wrangell, 66
Wyoming, 96

RECOMMENDATIONS
for readers interested in northern history

Accidental Adventurer: Memoir of the First Women to Climb Mt. McKinley, Barbara Washburn, paperback, $16.95

Amazing Pipeline Stories: How Building the Trans-Alaska Pipeline Transformed Life in America's Last Frontier, Dermot Cole, paperback, $14.95

Arctic Bush Pilot, Jim Rearden and Andy Anderson, paperback, $17.95

Crude Dreams: A Personal History of Oil & Politics in Alaska, Jack Roderick, paperback, $24.95

George Carmack: Man of Mystery Who Set off the Klondike Gold Rush, James Albert Johnson, paperback, $14.95

Good Time Girls of the Alaska-Yukon Gold Rush, Lael Morgan, paperback, $17.95

Kay Fanning's Alaska Story, Kay Fanning, paperback, $17.95

North to the Future: The Story of Alaska Statehood, 1959-2009, Dermot Cole, paperback, $15.95

North to Wolf Country: My Life among the Creatures of Alaska, James W. Brooks, paperback, $17.95

Saving for the Future: My Life & the Alaska Permanent Fund, Dave Rose, paperback $17.95

Sarah: How a Hockey Mom Turned Alaska's Political Establishment Upside Down, Kaylene Johnson, hardbound, $19.95

The Spill: Personal Stories of the Exxon Valdez Disaster, Sharon Bushell & Stan Jones, paperback, $17.95

Tales of Alaska's Bush Rat Governor, Jay Hammond, paperback, $17.95

Look for these titles in your local bookstore or order them online at www.EpicenterPress.com.

EPICENTER PRESS
Alaska Book Adventures™
www.EpicenterPress.com

"ART and ESKIMO POWER"

The Life and Times of HOWARD ROCK
by Lael Morgan
Epicenter Press

Prior to his birth in 1911, a shaman predicted that Howard Rock would be a great man. Raised in a harshly primitive hunting society in Point Hope, Alaska, the Eskimo turned his back on his homeland for nearly half a century to make a name for himself as an artist in Oregon and Washington states. But when he learned the village of his birth had been chosen by the Atomic Energy Commission for a dangerous nuclear experiment, he returned to defend his people with extraordinary decisiveness and skill as a crusading newspaper editor.
260 pp. 32 pp., black and white photos.

What readers are saying about the book...

"Howard Rock was an artist, a crusading editor, and a fierce, articulate, and effective advocate for his people. He was a national treasure, and Lael Morgan's colorful, involving account of his life deserves a mutual audience."

RICHARD NIXON

"Art and Eskimo Power: The Life and Times of Alaskan Howard Rock will stand as a monument to a Man, a time and an issue. It is written and presented with intelligence and knowledge. In keeping with the tradition of Howard Rock, Lael Morgan has presented this book as journalism with affection."

WILBUR E. GARRETT, Editor
NATIONAL GEOGRAPHIC

ORDER FORM

QTY.	TITLE	TOTAL
_____	"Art and Eskimo Power" (clothbound) $24.95	_____
_____	"Art and Eskimo Power" (paper) $16.95	_____
	OTHER BOOKS BY EPICENTER PRESS:	
_____	"Four Generations on the Yukon" $15.95	_____
_____	"Steamboats on the Chena" $9.95	_____

Please include $2.50 postage and handling for one title and $1.25 for each additional title.

Add postage/handling _____

TOTAL PURCHASE _____

NAME _____

ADDRESS _____

CITY _____

STATE _____ ZIP _____

☐ VISA   ☐ MASTERCARD # _____

Signature _____ Exp. Date _____

Send to: EPICENTER PRESS, P.O. BOX 60529, Fairbanks, AK 99706

www.ingramcontent.com/pod-product-compliance
Lightning Source LLC
Chambersburg PA
CBHW011147290426
44109CB00023B/2526